Codependency and Narcissistic Abuse Recovery Guide

Cure Your Codependent & Narcissist Personality Disorder and Relationships! Follow The Ultimate User Manual for Healing Narcissism & Codependence NOW!

By Victoria Hoffman

"Codependency and Narcissistic Abuse Recovery Guide: Cure Your Codependent & Narcissist Personality Disorder and Relationships! Follow The Ultimate User Manual for Healing Narcissism & Codependence NOW!" Written by "By Victoria Hoffman".

Codependency and Narcissistic Abuse Recovery Guide is a set of the books "Codependency Recovery Guide" & "Narcissistic Abuse Healing Guide".

Hope You Enjoy!

Table of Contents

Codependency Recovery Guide

Table of Contents
Codependency Recovery Guide
Introduction
Chapter 1 – Are you Codependent?

> The Traits of Codependency
> How Codependency Develops

Codependency Tests
Chapter 2 – Revisiting Your Past

> Dysfunctional Families
> Addiction
> Illnesses

Chapter 3 – The Recovery Process

> Setting Boundaries
> Putting Yourself First
> Listen to Others
> Validation

Chapter 4 – Break the Patterns

> Denial
> Low Self-Esteem
> Compliance
> Control
> Avoidance
> Recovery Reminders

Conclusion
Narcissistic Abuse Healing Guide
Introduction
Chapter 1: Success Stories

Introduction to Narcissistic Characters
Success Stories of Narcissistic Abuse

    Case Study #1: Lilie's Experience with a Narcissistic Husband
    Case Study #2: Kelly Detaches Herself from Her Narcissistic Family

Chapter 2: Victim Mode

  What Makes It Hard to Heal from A Narcissistic Abuse

    The Clarity in Retrospect
    Learned powerlessness
    The Lonely Road
    Fear of the Unknown
    Laying Down the Facts
    Don't Expect Them to Change

  The Cornerstone of Healing

    Ask Why
    Be Specific
    Be Kind to Yourself
    Be Smart
    Stay on Top

Chapter 3: Getting Rid of The Pseudo Personality

  How to Acknowledge Your Pseudo Personality?
  The Challenges of Dealing with a Pseudo Personality

    Understanding Their Fragile Ego Could Be a Major Challenge
    Comprehending Their Ability to Shift Gears from the Real to the False World
    The Pseudo Personality Is Pretty Controlling
    It May Be Challenging to Identify the Nitty-Gritty of a Pseudo Personality

A Pseudo Personality Is a Professional Liar
It May Be Difficult to Deal with Their Vicious Temper
The Pseudo Personality Will Always Play a Victim

Breaking the Machination

Refuse to Engage with an Individual Who Has a Pseudo Personality
Establish If the Conversation Must Always Be Spearheaded by Them
Understand That They Are Takers and Not Givers Most of the Time

Chapter 4 – Inner Child Healing

How Does It Happen?
The Inner Child in Adulthood
What Does a Stable Childhood Look Like?
Caring for Your Inner Child

Identifying Childhood Pain
Re-Parenting Your Inner Child
Engaging Your Inner Child

Chapter 5: Creating Your Thoughts

Awareness
Hearing of the Inner Voice
5 Steps to Regain Control of Your Thoughts

1. Study How to Prevent Your Thoughts
2. Recognize Negative Feelings Within You
3. Note down Your Mental Tape
4. Get the Lie
5. Find the Truth

Get Rid of The Poor Self-Concept of Your Thoughts

Live in the Moment
Create Awareness

Inscribe in a Journal
Don't Judge
Be Connected to Yourself
Enhance Watchful Meditation
Have Participation in Your Personal Life
Advanced Beginner's Mind
Let Go
Have Compassion to Yourself

Refocus Your Mind

Begin by Assessing your Mental Focus
Eradicate Interferences
Put Your Focus on One Thing at a Time
Be in the Moment
Exercise Mindfulness
Take a Small Break
Practice More to Strengthen Your Focus

Tips for Improving Mindfulness

1. Just Respire
2. Have a Walk
3. Enjoy Being in Silence

How to Affirm Yourself

1. Remove Selfish and Cynical Individuals in Your Life
2. Have Goals and Achieve Them
3. Expand Yourself
4. Have Time to Assist Others

Chapter 6: Survival Mode

Is it PTSD?
How Can You Tell if You Have C-PTSD?

Intrusive depressing thoughts
Stress

- Avoidance
- Exclusion
- Changes in Arousal and Reactivity
- Difficulty Controlling Emotions
- Altered Perception of Self and World
- Obsession with the Abuser
- Difficulty with Personal Relationships

Getting Help

- Finding a Support Group
- Identify Early Warning Triggers
- Identify Coping Methods

Psychotherapy
Cognitive-Behavioral Therapy
Medications
Gratitude Exercises

- Appreciate Yourself
- Keep a Gratitude Journal
- Schedule a Gratitude Visit
- Make a Gratitude Jar
- Laugh Out Loud
- Make a Daily Goal
- Find a Gratitude Buddy
- Reduce Your Complaints
- Act of Kindness
- Gratitude Prompts
- Make a Collage

Chapter 7: Thriving Mode

- Set Boundaries
- Be Assertive
- Know Your Rights
- Be Strategic

- Check for Abuse
- Check Your Silence
- Check Your Anger
- Check for Their Willingness to Change
- Be Aware of Manipulation
- Honesty to Yourself

- Be Educative
- Confront Abuse Effectively
- Have Consequences
- Get Support and Purpose Elsewhere
- Trust Your Intuition

Chapter 8- Getting into a New Relationship

Signs You Are Ready for a New Relationship

- You Don't Think About Them Anymore
- You Have No Hatred for Them
- When You Can Open up Freely
- You Don't Stalk Them Anymore
- You Don't Feel Wrong About Your past Experiences
- You Have No Fear of Falling for a Similar Person Again
- You Take Care of Yourself
- You Are Ready to Take the Risk Again
- You Genuinely Want to Start a New Relationship

Redefining Sexy After a Narcissistic Relationship

- Don't Think You Are Unattractive; Make Yourself Attractive Instead
- Don't Let Your past Relationship Affect Your Current Life
- Find Your Confidence
- Dress Well and Give Yourself a Treat
- Maintain the Right Posture
- Learn the Skills of a Good Romance
- Love Yourself and Your Life

How to Become Your Own Source of Happiness?

    Make Yourself a Priority
    Do the Little Things You Love More Often
    Challenge Yourself by Doing Something New
    Get Enough Sleep
    Do the Workouts

How to Stay Single and Blessed

    Learn to Do Things on Your Own
    Develop Other Relationships
    Meet New People
    Treat Yourself
    Maintain a Supportive, Positive Company

Conclusion

Book2 title, subtitle and contents pages

Table of Contents
Codependency Recovery Guide
Introduction
Chapter 1 – Are you Codependent?

    The Traits of Codependency
    How Codependency Develops

Codependency Tests
Chapter 2 – Revisiting Your Past

    Dysfunctional Families
    Addiction
    Illnesses

Chapter 3 – The Recovery Process

    Setting Boundaries

Putting Yourself First
Listen to Others
Validation

Chapter 4 – Break the Patterns

Denial
Low Self-Esteem
Compliance
Control
Avoidance
Recovery Reminders

Conclusion
Narcissistic Abuse Healing Guide
Introduction
Chapter 1: Success Stories

Introduction to Narcissistic Characters
Success Stories of Narcissistic Abuse

Case Study #1: Lilie's Experience with a Narcissistic Husband
Case Study #2: Kelly Detaches Herself from Her Narcissistic Family

Chapter 2: Victim Mode

What Makes It Hard to Heal from A Narcissistic Abuse

The Clarity in Retrospect
Learned powerlessness
The Lonely Road
Fear of the Unknown
Laying Down the Facts
Don't Expect Them to Change

The Cornerstone of Healing

Ask Why

  Be Specific
  Be Kind to Yourself
  Be Smart
  Stay on Top

Chapter 3: Getting Rid of The Pseudo Personality

How to Acknowledge Your Pseudo Personality?
The Challenges of Dealing with a Pseudo Personality

  Understanding Their Fragile Ego Could Be a Major Challenge
  Comprehending Their Ability to Shift Gears from the Real to the False World
  The Pseudo Personality Is Pretty Controlling
  It May Be Challenging to Identify the Nitty-Gritty of a Pseudo Personality
  A Pseudo Personality Is a Professional Liar
  It May Be Difficult to Deal with Their Vicious Temper
  The Pseudo Personality Will Always Play a Victim

Breaking the Machination

  Refuse to Engage with an Individual Who Has a Pseudo Personality
  Establish If the Conversation Must Always Be Spearheaded by Them
  Understand That They Are Takers and Not Givers Most of the Time

Chapter 4 – Inner Child Healing

How Does It Happen?
The Inner Child in Adulthood
What Does a Stable Childhood Look Like?
Caring for Your Inner Child

  Identifying Childhood Pain
  Re-Parenting Your Inner Child

Engaging Your Inner Child

Chapter 5: Creating Your Thoughts

Awareness
Hearing of the Inner Voice
5 Steps to Regain Control of Your Thoughts

1. Study How to Prevent Your Thoughts
2. Recognize Negative Feelings Within You
3. Note down Your Mental Tape
4. Get the Lie
5. Find the Truth

Get Rid of The Poor Self-Concept of Your Thoughts

Live in the Moment
Create Awareness
Inscribe in a Journal
Don't Judge
Be Connected to Yourself
Enhance Watchful Meditation
Have Participation in Your Personal Life
Advanced Beginner's Mind
Let Go
Have Compassion to Yourself

Refocus Your Mind

Begin by Assessing your Mental Focus
Eradicate Interferences
Put Your Focus on One Thing at a Time
Be in the Moment
Exercise Mindfulness
Take a Small Break
Practice More to Strengthen Your Focus

Tips for Improving Mindfulness

1. Just Respire
2. Have a Walk
3. Enjoy Being in Silence

How to Affirm Yourself

1. Remove Selfish and Cynical Individuals in Your Life
2. Have Goals and Achieve Them
3. Expand Yourself
4. Have Time to Assist Others

Chapter 6: Survival Mode

Is it PTSD?
How Can You Tell if You Have C-PTSD?

Intrusive depressing thoughts
Stress
Avoidance
Exclusion
Changes in Arousal and Reactivity
Difficulty Controlling Emotions
Altered Perception of Self and World
Obsession with the Abuser
Difficulty with Personal Relationships

Getting Help

Finding a Support Group
Identify Early Warning Triggers
Identify Coping Methods

Psychotherapy
Cognitive-Behavioral Therapy
Medications
Gratitude Exercises

Appreciate Yourself
Keep a Gratitude Journal

- Schedule a Gratitude Visit
- Make a Gratitude Jar
- Laugh Out Loud
- Make a Daily Goal
- Find a Gratitude Buddy
- Reduce Your Complaints
- Act of Kindness
- Gratitude Prompts
- Make a Collage

Chapter 7: Thriving Mode

- Set Boundaries
- Be Assertive
- Know Your Rights
- Be Strategic
  - Check for Abuse
  - Check Your Silence
  - Check Your Anger
  - Check for Their Willingness to Change
  - Be Aware of Manipulation
  - Honesty to Yourself
- Be Educative
- Confront Abuse Effectively
- Have Consequences
- Get Support and Purpose Elsewhere
- Trust Your Intuition

Chapter 8 - Getting into a New Relationship

Signs You Are Ready for a New Relationship

- You Don't Think About Them Anymore
- You Have No Hatred for Them
- When You Can Open up Freely
- You Don't Stalk Them Anymore

You Don't Feel Wrong About Your past Experiences
You Have No Fear of Falling for a Similar Person Again
You Take Care of Yourself
You Are Ready to Take the Risk Again
You Genuinely Want to Start a New Relationship

Redefining Sexy After a Narcissistic Relationship

Don't Think You Are Unattractive; Make Yourself Attractive Instead
Don't Let Your past Relationship Affect Your Current Life
Find Your Confidence
Dress Well and Give Yourself a Treat
Maintain the Right Posture
Learn the Skills of a Good Romance
Love Yourself and Your Life

How to Become Your Own Source of Happiness?

Make Yourself a Priority
Do the Little Things You Love More Often
Challenge Yourself by Doing Something New
Get Enough Sleep
Do the Workouts

How to Stay Single and Blessed

Learn to Do Things on Your Own
Develop Other Relationships
Meet New People
Treat Yourself
Maintain a Supportive, Positive Company

Conclusion

Codependency Recovery Guide

Cure your Codependent Personality & Relationships with this No More Codependence User Manual, Heal from Narcissists & Sociopathic People by Learning How to Take Back Control

By Victoria Hoffman

Introduction

Congratulations on purchasing the *Codependency Recovery Guide* and thank you for doing so.

The following chapters will discuss the different approaches towards recovering from a codependent relationship and the best ways of rebuilding your life once again. There are lots of practical examples that can be followed to help an individual recover from a bad relationship or rebuild their existing love.

There are plenty of books on this subject on the market, thanks again for choosing this one! Every effort was made to ensure it is full of as much useful information as possible, please enjoy it!

Chapter 1 – Are you Codependent?

Codependency is a dysfunctional relationship where an individual relies on the other(s) for their emotional and passionate needs. It likewise portrays a relationship that empowers someone else to keep up their flippant, addictive, or underachieving conduct.

Do you feel caught in your relationship? Is it accurate to say that you are the one that is always making sacrifices in your relationship? At that point, you might be in a codependent relationship.

The term codependency has been around for a considerable length of time. In spite of the fact that it initially applied to life partners of heavy drinkers (first called co-drunkards), specialists uncovered that the attributes of codependents were considerably more pervasive in the all-inclusive community than had recently envisioned. Truth be told, they found that if you were brought up in a dysfunctional family or had an evil parent, you could likewise be codependent.

Specialists likewise found that codependent side effects deteriorated if left untreated. Fortunately, they're reversible.

Manifestations of Codependency

Coming up next is a rundown of indications of codependency and being in a codependent relationship. You do not need them all to qualify as codependent.

Dysfunctional correspondence. Codependents experience difficulty with regard to imparting their considerations, emotions, and requirements. Obviously, if you do not have a clue of what you think, feel, or need, this turns into an issue. You are hesitant to be honest, on the grounds that you would prefer not to annoy another person. Communication winds up untrustworthy and confounding when you attempt to control the other individual out of dread.

Poor limits. Limits are kind of a nonexistent line among you and others. It splits what's yours and someone else's, and that applies not exclusively to your body, cash, and possessions, but also to your emotions, contemplations, and necessities. That is particularly hard for codependents. They have foggy or frail limits. They feel in charge of other individuals' emotions and issues or fault their very own on another person. Some codependents have inflexible limits. They are deterred and pulled back, making it difficult for other individuals to draw near to them. Some of the time, individuals flip to and fro between having feeble limits and having inflexible ones.

Rejection. One of the issues individuals face in getting help for codependency is that they're trying to claim ignorance about it, implying that they do not confront their concern. Typically, they think the issue is another person or the circumstance. They either continue whining or attempting to fix the other individual or move between various relationships or jobs and never confess up the way that they have an issue. Codependents likewise deny their sentiments and necessities. Frequently, they do not have the foggiest idea of what they're feeling and are rather centered around what others are feeling. Something very similar goes for their needs. They focus on other individuals' needs and not their own. They may be trying to claim ignorance of their requirement for space and self-governance. Albeit some codependents appear to be penniless, others act like they're independent with regards to requiring help. They will not connect and experience difficulty getting attention. They are willfully ignorant of their helplessness and requirement for adoration and closeness.

Reactivity. A result of poor limits is that you respond to everybody's contemplations and emotions. If somebody says something you cannot help contradicting, you either trust it or become protective. You ingest their words, on the grounds that there is no limit. With a limit, you would understand it was only their assessment and not an impression of you and not feel compromised by differences.

Caretaking. Another impact of poor limits is that if another person has an issue, you need to push them to the point that you surrender yourself. It is normal to feel compassion toward somebody, however, codependents start putting other individuals in front of themselves. Indeed, they have to help and may feel rejected if someone else doesn't need assistance. In addition, they continue attempting to help and fix the other individual, notwithstanding when that individual unmistakably is not taking their recommendation.

Low confidence. Feeling that you are bad enough or contrasting yourself with others are indications of low confidence. The dubious thing about confidence is that a few people have a favorable opinion of themselves, yet, it is just a mask — they really feel unlovable or lacking. Underneath, typically avoided cognizance, are sentiments of disgrace. Blame and hairsplitting regularly oblige low confidence. If everything is immaculate, you do not feel terrible about yourself.

Control. Control helps codependents have a sense of security. Everybody needs some authority over occasions in their life. You wouldn't have any desire to live in steady vulnerability and disorder, however, for codependents, control restrains their capacity to go out on a limb and offer their sentiments. Some of the time, they have an addiction that either causes them to extricate up, similar to liquor abuse, or encourages them to hold their emotions down, similar to workaholism, with the goal that they do not show it. Codependents additionally need to control those near them, since they need other individuals to carry on with a particular goal in mind to feel OK. It is possible to have programs that help individuals understand how to control themselves. Then again, codependents are bossy and reveal to you what you ought to or shouldn't do. This is an infringement of another person's limit.

Difficult feelings. Codependency makes pressure and prompts agonizing feelings. Disgrace and low confidence make uneasiness and dread about being judged, dismissed, committing errors, being a disappointment, and feeling caught by being close or being separated from everyone else. Different side effects lead to sentiments of indignation and disdain, despondency, misery, and hopelessness. At the point when the emotions are excessive, you can feel numb.

Satisfying others. It is fine to need to satisfy somebody you care about, however, codependents ordinarily do not think they have a decision. Saying "No" causes them uneasiness. Some codependents experience serious difficulties saying "No" to anybody. They make a special effort and sacrifice their own needs to suit other individuals.

Reliance. Codependents need other individuals to like them to feel okay about themselves. They're anxious about being rejected or deserted, regardless of whether they can work individually. There are people who constantly need the approval of others even when it is better to think for themselves. This quality makes it difficult for them to cut off an association even when a relationship is not working out for them.

Issues with closeness. By this, it is the problems associated with being intimate with your partner. I'm looking at being open and close with somebody in a private relationship. As a result of feeling afraid, you may expect that you'll be judged, rejected, or left. Some people feel that their partners are way more sophisticated than them and, in turn, fear to share their actual lives with them. This is a serious problem that can persist for a long time in a relationship and cause unexpected damage.

There is help for recuperation and change for individuals who are codependent. The initial step is getting direction from a close friend or family member and get the process started. It is better to do it immediately than wait.

The Traits of Codependency

Think about codependency—when two individuals with dysfunctional characteristics become more terrible together. Enmeshment happens when clear limits about where you start and where your partner finishes are not plainly characterized.

Think about the most despondent couple you have at any point met. (Ideally, you are not a piece of this pair.) You may ask why these individuals are still attached. Grown-ups are willing members in organizations. What's more, as unfortunate as connections might be, there can be gains for the two gatherings. Basic purposes behind staying together incorporate youngsters, accounts, time contributed, and dread of the disgrace that may accompany separating. Yet, the greater issue is the conviction that one or the two individuals accept they have the right to be abused.

Indications of Codependency

The customary meaning of codependency has concentrated on control, support, and upkeep of associations with people who are artificially reliant, or participating in unfortunate practices, for example, narcissism. An exemplary codependency model is an alcoholic spouse and his empowering wife.

Scientists contend that codependent people share the duty regarding the unfortunate conduct, principally by concentrating their lives on the wiped out or the terrible conduct and by making their very own confidence and prosperity depend upon the conduct of the undesirable relative.

Different scientists guessed that the practical (or sound) partner supports the distressed partner when the individual takes part in unwanted conduct. This conduct is at last wonderful to the distressed partner, which serves to fortify it. The partner who controls the most rewards (which manufactures their capacity base) is thought to be the amazing one, while the other is obliged to the person in question. At whatever point there is progressing struggle, there is basic understanding. As such, it takes two to tango, and the needy or subservient partner may not be as powerless, aloof, or blameless as they show up.

The accompanying inquiries can fill in as a manual to decide whether your relationship includes codependency:

- Do you spread your partner's issues with medications, liquor, or the law?
- Does your feeling of direction include making outrageous sacrifices to fulfill your partner's needs?
- Do you stay silent to maintain a strategic distance from contentions?
- Do you continually stress over others' assessments of you?
- Do you feel caught in your relationship?
- Is it difficult to state no when your partner makes requests on your time and life?

The Development of Codependency

During childbirth, we are characteristically helpless and totally subject to our guardians for nourishment, security, and guideline. A newborn child's connection and clinging to at least one parental figure is basic for physical and enthusiastic survival. This basic connection makes the newborn child dependent on the necessities and vulnerabilities of the parental figure.

Growing up with a problematic or inaccessible parent means assuming the job of overseer and additionally empowering agent. A youngster, in this circumstance, puts the parent's needs first.

Dysfunctional families do not recognize that issues exist. Accordingly, its individuals quell feelings and neglect their own needs to concentrate on the necessities of the inaccessible parent(s). At the point when the "parentified" youngster turns into a grown-up, the individual in question rehashes a similar dynamic in their grown-up connections.

Disdain fabricates when you do not perceive your very own wants and needs. A typical conduct inclination is to blow up or lash out when your partner allows you to down. Coming up short on an interior locus of control means looking for outer wellsprings of approval and control. You may attempt to control your partner's practices so you can feel OK. You may act bombastic and bossy, and make irrational requests on your partner. Furthermore, when you understand you cannot control their dispositions or activities you become disillusioned, and may slide into a discouraged state.

It tends to be difficult to recognize an individual who is codependent and one who is simply tenacious or fascinated with someone else. Be that as it may, an individual who is codependent will typically:

- Remain in the relationship regardless of whether they know that their partner does destructive things.

- Discover no fulfillment or joy in life outside of getting things done for the other individual.

- Utilize all their time and vitality to give their partner all that they request.

- Overlook their own ethics or inner voice to do what the other individual needs.

- Feel consistent nervousness about their relationship because of their longing to consistently be fulfilling to the other individual.

- Do anything to please and fulfill their empowering agent regardless of the cost to themselves.

- Other individuals may attempt to converse with the codependent about their worries. In any case, regardless of whether others propose that the individual is excessively needy, an individual in a codependent relationship will think that it is difficult to leave the relationship.

- Feel regretful about considering themselves in the relationship and will not express any needs or wants.

- The codependent individual will feel extraordinary clash about isolating themselves from the empowering agent on the grounds that their own character is focused after sacrificing themselves for the other individual.

How Codependency Develops

Codependency is something that can be passed down from one generation to another. It is a passionate and conduct condition that influences a person's capacity to have a sound, commonly fulfilling relationship. It is otherwise called "relationship addiction" since individuals with codependency frequently structure or keep up connections that are uneven, sincerely damaging as well as injurious. The turmoil was first identified around ten years back as the aftereffect of long periods of considering relational connections in groups of drunkards. Mutually dependent conduct is found out by watching and impersonating other relatives who show this sort of conduct.

Who Does Co-Dependency Affect?

Codependency frequently influences a life partner, a parent, kin, companion, or collaborator of an individual harassed with liquor or medication reliance. Initially, mutually dependent was a term used to depict partners in concoction reliance, people living with, or in an association with an addicted individual. Comparative examples have been found in individuals involved with incessantly or rationally sick people. Today, be that as it may, the term has expanded to portray any mutually dependent individual from any dysfunctional family.

What is a Dysfunctional Family and How does it Lead to Co-Dependency?

A dysfunctional family is one in which individuals experience the ill effects of dread, outrage, torment, or disgrace that is overlooked or denied. Basic issues may incorporate any of the accompanyings:

- An addiction by a relative to drugs, liquor, connections, work, nourishment, sex, or betting.

- The presence of physical, passionate, or sexual maltreatment.

- The nearness of a relative experiencing a constant mental or physical disease.

Dysfunctional families do not recognize that issues exist. They do not discuss them or defy them. Thus, relatives figure out how to curb feelings and dismiss their own needs. They become "survivors." They create practices that help them deny, disregard, or maintain a strategic distance from difficult feelings. They separate themselves. They do not talk. They do not contact. They do not stand up to. They do not feel. They do not trust. The character and enthusiastic improvement of the individuals from a dysfunctional family are regularly repressed.

Consideration and vitality center around the relative who is sick or addicted. The mutually dependent individual ordinarily sacrifices their needs to deal with an individual who is wiped out. At the point when mutually dependent people place other individuals' wellbeing, welfare, and security before their own, they can lose contact with their very own needs, wants, and feelings of self.

How Do Co-dependent People Behave?

Mutually dependent people have low confidence and search for anything outside of themselves to make them feel good. They think that it is difficult to "act naturally." Some attempt to feel better through liquor, medications, or nicotine - and become addicted. Others may create habitual practices like workaholism, betting, or aimless sexual movement.

They mean well. They attempt to deal with an individual who is encountering difficulty, yet the caretaking ends up being intriguing. Mutually dependent people regularly take on a saint's job and become "supporters" to a person out of luck. A wife may cover for her alcoholic spouse; a mother may rationalize a truant tyke; or a dad may "pull a few strings" to shield his youngster from enduring the results of reprobate conduct.

The issue is that these rehashed salvage endeavors enable the penniless individual to proceed on a dangerous course and to turn out to be much progressively subject to the undesirable caretaking of the "supporter." As this dependence builds, the mutually dependent builds up a feeling of remuneration and fulfillment from "being required." When the caretaking ends up urgent, the mutually dependent feels choiceless and vulnerable in the relationship, however, it cannot split away from the cycle of conduct that causes it. Mutually dependent people see themselves as exploited people and are pulled in to that equivalent shortcoming in the affection and fellowship connections.

Qualities of Co-Dependent People are:

- A feeling of blame when championing themselves
- Lying/unscrupulousness
- Difficulty deciding
- An inclination to confound love and pity, with the propensity to "love" individuals they can pity and save
- An unfortunate reliance on connections. The mutually dependent will effectively clutch a relationship; to maintain a strategic distance from the sentiment of surrender
- Issues with closeness/limits
- An outrageous requirement for endorsement and acknowledgment
- A convincing need to control others
- Absence of trust in self and additionally others
- A misrepresented awareness of other's expectations for the activities of others
- The dread of being deserted or alone
- Difficulty identifying sentiments
- An inclination to wind up hurt when individuals do not perceive their endeavors
- Unbending nature/difficulty acclimating to change
- Incessant annoyance
- A propensity to accomplish more than their offer, constantly
- Poor correspondences

How Is Co-Dependency Treated?

Since codependency is typically established in an individual's adolescence, treatment regularly includes an investigation into early youth issues and their relationship to current ruinous personal conduct standards. Treatment incorporates instruction, experiential gatherings, and individual and gathering treatment through which mutually dependent people rediscover themselves and identify foolish standards of conduct. Treatment likewise centers around helping patients connect with sentiments that have been covered during adolescence and on reproducing relational peculiarities. The objective is to enable them to encounter their full scope of sentiments once more.

The initial phase in changing undesirable conduct is to get it. It is significant for mutually dependent people and their relatives to teach themselves about the course and cycle of addiction and how it stretches out into their connections. Libraries, medication, and liquor misuse treatment focus and psychological well-being focus frequently offer instructive materials and projects to people in general.

A great deal of progress and development is essential for mutually dependent and their family. Any caretaking conduct that permits or empowers maltreatment to proceed in the family should be perceived and halted. The mutually dependent must identify and grasp their sentiments and requirements. This may incorporate figuring out how to state "no," to cherish yet intense, and figuring out how to act naturally dependent. Individuals discover opportunity, love, and peacefulness in their recuperation.

Expectation lies in finding out additional. The more you comprehend codependency, the better you can adapt to its belongings. Connecting for information and help can enable somebody to carry on with a more beneficial, all the more satisfying life.

Codependency Tests

Codependency may mean somewhat different things to different individuals, yet basically, it is the point at which one individual is sacrificing more for their relationship than the other.

In sentimental connections, it is the point at which one partners needs over-the-top consideration and mental help, and frequently this is joined forces with them having a disease or an addiction which makes them considerably progressively reliant.

A codependent couple will not be beneficial for one another. For the most part, they will get together in light of the fact that either of them has a dysfunctional character, and as a rule, they will aggravate one another.

For instance, individuals engaged with narcissists will wind up giving and giving, yet it is rarely enough. Their partner will continue moving the goal lines and making unreasonable requests until the unfortunate casualty is totally worn out.

It is imperative to recollect that in a sound relationship, it is entirely expected to rely upon your partner for solace and backing. Be that as it may, there is a harmony between each partner's capacity to be autonomous and their capacity to appreciate common assistance, and if that parity is off, that is when things get muddled.

We approached different relationship specialists for the signs you could be in a codependent relationship. This is what they stated:

1. You need to 'fix' your partner

Everything begins as a fantasy, yet then your new partner begins to give a few indications of undesirable practices. Do you wind up making every one of the sacrifices to help your partner? Do you have an inclination that you lost yourself and you need the endorsement of your partner to be whole? Sound connections are made when the two partners have shared regard, trust, and are constantly fair with each other. Codependent characters will, in general, be accommodating people, blossoming from helping other people (or notwithstanding figuring they may 'fix' them). When thinking about someone else prevents you from having your very own needs met or if your self-esteem is reliant on being needed, you might head down the codependent way.

2. You have to request endorsement

If you believe you regularly need to get endorsement or authorization to do fundamental ordinary living, or if you believe you cannot settle on a basic choice without that individual, that could be an early indication of a codependent relationship. If you enter an association with heaps of certainty yet after some time, you start to question yourself, your self-esteem, and you are less definitive, you could be in a damaging narcissistic codependent relationship. If you have been constrained by your partner or they request being the essential chief in the relationship, at that point when you separate, you could even now accept and feel you need them.

It might be difficult to rationally isolate yourself from that perspective or even the routine of the relationship, yet when you can mend and better self-care, you can start to concentrate more on your needs and being a superior adaptation of yourself.

3. You lose contact with companions or family

I think when you start losing contact with the individuals who are imperative to you, it is a sign something is not exactly right. You start seeing that your essential center is the other individual, yet to the point where you are truly winding up very confined from individuals who were already significant. That being stated, I believe it is entirely ordinary when individuals begin to look all starry eyed at, for every other person to feel out of view. In any case, when it continues for some time, that is a noticeable sign you are getting to be unmoored from the grapples in your life that keep you consistent and keep you on the track which you have been on.

I think we should be extremely aware of that on the grounds that else we become progressively codependent on our partners, at that point, if you choose they aren't beneficial for you, you glance around and there are no companions, no leisure activities, and the world has turned into this one partner you have currently chosen is not right. In any case, presently leaving that partner, you are sacrificing the relationship, as well as life, since you have nothing else.

4. You are continually searching for consolation

How would you know if your relationship is codependent? Ask yourself these inquiries:

• Do both of you rationalize the other's awful or ill-bred conduct, or maintain a strategic distance from direct discussions about the condition of the relationship?

• Do you or your partner characterize yourselves by the relationship? Do you experience issues being separated from everyone else?

• Are you or your partner constantly stressed that the other will sever the relationship?

• Do you or your partner demonstration coquettishly with individuals outside of the relationship to make the different envious, or take steps to leave to make sure you can be asked to remain?

• Do both of you need consistent confirmation that you are cherished?

• Is there a ton of strain or power in your relationship, and do both of you subtly appreciate the 'show' of successive separations and reunions?

• Do you or your partner think of little tests to get consideration from the other?

5. You lose every one of your limits

One method for taking a gander at a codependent individual is if she is an over-provider. She generally feels excessively in charge of somebody or thinks about somebody. She truly feels like she needs to continue giving and giving, and overcompensating. These ladies can be extremely solid, yet the issue is they do not get a handle on the requirement for limits. Limits are entirely helpful with individuals you care about, yet in a codependent individual's heart, 'limits' is a grimy word. They think 'the minute I care about you, I drop every one of my limits. I let you ignore me since I trust you have a story, so I over-clarify away each and everything for you.' as such, you give more confidence to their story than to yours. You must have firm limits, since when you do not have them, or you are not mindful of them, you fall into the codependent trap.

6. You do not feel like you have your very own free life

In any relationship, it is imperative to both bond with your partner, yet in addition, keep up your very own life. You would prefer not to turn out to be so reliant on another person that you lose what your identity is, or that substance that makes you extraordinary. How would you keep up the two sides of yourself? Schedule date nights as well as evenings with companions or evenings alone to loosen up. At the start of a relationship, there is undeniable value in not going through consistently together and allowing yourselves to miss each other. Also, when you are getting things done alone, you become an all the more intriguing, balanced individual. In this way, a superior partner to anybody.

7. You start filling in the holes

The principal indication of codependency crawling into a relationship will include one individual beginning to assume on the liability to stay in contact and interface. As an partner pulls back in how much time, exertion, and care they are giving, the other partner intuitively fills in the hole by working harder to remain fortified. When this occurs, the relationship has shifted an undesirable way towards codependency.

8. Your partner has unfortunate propensities

One early indication of a codependent relationship (utilizing the primary meaning of an 'empowering agent') is the point at which one individual more than once takes part in an unfortunate conduct, for example, reliably drinking until they go out or pigging out until they feel wiped out, and the other individual either goes along with them in it, despite the fact that the individual doesn't really prefer to drink or voraciously consume food, or supports it for their own reasons.

If you addressed 'Yes' to even a couple of these inquiries, you are likely in a codependent relationship.

Chapter 2 – Revisiting Your Past

Dysfunctional Families

The expression "dysfunctional family," when utilized distinctly by experts, has turned out to be a prevalent language in America where dysfunctional families are the standard because of social qualities, a high separation rate, and broad addictions – from doctor-prescribed medications to working out, working, and shopping.

A sound family is a place of refuge – a position of sustenance and sustaining – that has a demeanor of receptiveness, immediacy, and liveliness, and takes into consideration the opportunity of articulation. There might be infrequent contentions and articulations of annoyance, yet harmony returns and people feel cherished and regarded. It works easily like a well-run organization. The officials – the guardians – make and concur upon principles, which are reliable and sensible.

Jack Welch, the previous CEO of General Electric, changed an organization that had a shut, internal-centered attitude, an inept administration, and uncommunicative workers. He understood the significance of making every representative feel like an esteemed member whose voice made a difference and prided himself on having an "open entryway" strategy that supported opportunity of articulation. Welch democratized the organization, giving a great many workers standard chances to challenge their managers and offer their thoughts in basic leadership. This strengthening style came about in flooded execution and representative fulfillment. They felt some portion of a group and that their voice made a difference. He despised mystery and refusal, and needed issues confronted and unraveled. He needed representatives that were free masterminds and candid about their thoughts and convictions, notwithstanding when awkward – when it "may sting." Employees were given direct input – positive and negative – and they thus assessed their managers. He sorted out discussions and critical thinking training. G.E. was a model of an open framework both all around. It looked worldwide for new thoughts from different organizations and shared the learning it picked up, which propelled its providers.

Obviously, a family doesn't have the capacity to boost generation and benefit, yet you can promptly observe that Welch's thoughts of transparency, direct correspondence, and populism increases worker's confidence, which occurs in sound families. In dysfunctional families, individuals have lower confidence and will, in general, be codependent. A portion of the side effects are depicted beneath, yet not all are important to make brokenness.

1. Unconventionality. Individuals have a sense of security when family life is unsurprising. If kids never recognize what state of mind Mom or Dad will be in, they cannot be unconstrained and are constantly on edge. Far more atrocious is mayhem, where the family is in a consistent emergency, frequently because of addiction, psychological sickness, or sexual, physical, or psychological mistreatment. Rather than a place of refuge, the family turns into a combat area to getaway. Kids may create substantial grievances, similar to cerebral pains and stomach hurts.

2. Assertion and Inconsistency. What are more regrettable than unbending standards are self-assertive and conflicting guidelines. Kids never know when they'll be rebuffed. Standards that do not bode well are unfair. This is merciless and breeds learned powerlessness and fierceness that can never be communicated. Youngsters are in steady dread, tread lightly, and feel miserable and angry on account of the capriciousness and injustice. Their feeling

of worth and nobility is disregarded. They lose regard and trust in their folks and specialist all in all. Since they're compelled to consent, some carry on with defiant or reprobate conduct, by doing ineffectively in school, or by utilizing drugs.

3. Privileged insights. A few insider facts are kept for ages about a family disgrace – regardless of whether addiction, savagery, crime, sexual issues, or psychological instability. The disgrace is felt by youngsters – notwithstanding when they do not have a clue about the mystery.

4. Powerlessness to Problem-Solve. Settling issues and clashes is vital to a smooth-running association. Be that as it may, in dysfunctional families, youngsters and guardians are accused more than once of something very similar and there are consistent contentions or quiet dividers of hatred. Nothing gets settled.

Conversely, solid families are protected in light of the fact that open self-articulation is energized without judgment or reprisal. Love is indicated in words, however in empathic, sustaining, and strong conduct. Every member, down to the youngest, is treated as an esteemed, regarded part. Input is permitted, and there is a feeling of uniformity, regardless of whether guardians have the last veto. Guardians act mindfully and are responsible for their responsibilities and consider kids responsible for theirs. They right and rebuff trouble making, however, do not accuse their kids or assault their character. Slip-ups are permitted and excused, and guardians recognize their very own inadequacies. They energize and direct their youngsters and regard their protection and physical and passionate limits. These fixings manufacture confidence, trust, and uprightness.

5. Dysfunctional Communication. This can take numerous structures – from the nonattendance of correspondence to verbal

maltreatment. Talking is not equivalent to utilitarian correspondence, which includes tuning in, regard, decisiveness, and comprehension. In dysfunctional families, correspondence is neither confident nor open. Individuals do not tune in and verbal maltreatment prevails. Kids are reluctant to express their contemplations and emotions, and are frequently accused, disgraced, or chastened for self-articulation. They are advised legitimately or in a roundabout way not to feel what they feel and might be named a sissy, terrible, idiotic, languid, or childish. They learn not to scrutinize their folks and not to confide their observations and emotions.

6. Refusal. Forswearing is an approach to overlook or imagine that an excruciating reality doesn't exist. Guardians attempt to act typical in the midst of family issues and emergencies, for example, a parent's nonappearance, sickness, or liquor addiction. It never gets discussed, nor the issue illuminated. This makes kids question their observations and communicates something specific that they cannot discuss something bizarre and startling – even to one another.

7. Unbending Rules. In certain families where there is physical or dysfunctional behavior, guardians are excessively remiss or unreliable, youngsters need direction and do not have a sense of security and pondering. By and large, be that as it may, there are prohibitive and subjective standards. Many are implicit. There is no space for mix-ups. A few guardians assume control over choices that kids should make and control their interests, school courses, companions, and dress. Normal autonomy is viewed as traitorousness and deserting. They forbid discussing things regarded unseemly, for example, sex, passing, the holocaust, grandpa's limp, or that father was hitched previously. A few families have guidelines limiting the declaration of resentment, abundance, or crying. At the point when sentiments cannot be communicated,

youngsters learn restraint and become excessively controlled or controlling grown-ups, all adding to low-confidence.

8. Job Confusion. This happens when a parent is sincerely or physically missing or is unreliable and a kid takes on parental duties or turns into a buddy or compatriot to the next parent. This is habitually the situation after a separation, yet additionally occurs in unblemished families where guardians need closeness. This is age-improper and harming the kid mentally, who should now act like somewhat grown-up, subdue their needs and sentiments, and may feel that the individual is deceiving the other parent.

9. A Closed System. A shut family will not permit differing or new plans to be talked about among individuals or with strangers. Individuals aren't permitted to discuss the family to other people, and probably will not permit visitors from another race or religion. A few families are secluded and do not communicate with society. Others do, yet appearances are everything, and reality with regards to the family is not shared. At base are fears of unique thoughts and disgrace.

Today, organizations, youthful families, and countries are ending up increasingly open and populist – a confident sign for what's to come.

Addiction

Codependency is a condition where people endeavor and accept that if they control individuals, spots, and circumstances, they can infer a feeling of self-esteem. It takes after an addiction to dealing with the requirements and the issues of someone else. Truth be told, a considerable lot of the individuals I've worked with who are in these kinds of codependent connections end up inclination, by and large, what can be depicted as exemplary indications of addiction. A portion of the encounters they report include:

- Lifestyle changes
- On edge or neurotic intuition with no undeniable reason
- Changes as a part of their character as announced by loved ones
- Absence of inspiration or dormancy

In the wake of decision out that an individual is manhandling substances, for example, liquor or medicates, and discovering that their side effects are not indications of other enthusiastic or psychological well-being issues, I find what they are encountering is, truth be told, constant, dynamic, and backsliding addiction. In actuality, many who are in codependent connections basically turned out to be reliant on the individuals with whom they are seeing someone.

Negative feelings

In that capacity, many think that it is difficult to "quit" the relationship, much like an individual addicted to liquor experiences issues stopping drinking. The "relationship addiction" controls an individual's capacity to justify and settle on solid choices to their best advantage. Their lives end up being affected in a negative way because they are too reliant on another person for emotional support.

Four Key Strides to Codependency Recuperation

Finding a specialist who makes you feel good and safe is an incredible spot to start for any individual who wishes to change codependency problems. When getting past codependency problems, consider the following:

Creating information of what a sound relationship resembles: I never expect that an individual admitting and tolerating the addiction part of codependency requires some serious energy, and since it is a backsliding condition, urging individuals to keep on chipping away at their recuperation each day, in turn, is basic to their prosperity and possible mending. Experiencing codependency has a decent comprehension of what a solid relationship resembles. An aspect of my responsibilities is helping individuals comprehend what's in store in a sound relationship.

Codependency recuperation is a procedure: Many people who experience it have been rehearsing dysfunctional relationship aptitudes for the greater part of their lives. Conceding and tolerating the addiction segment of codependency requires some investment, and since it is a backsliding condition, urging individuals to keep on taking a shot at their recuperation each day is basic to their prosperity and possible mending.

Building up a sound feeling of self-identify: Like numerous individuals living with addiction, numerous individuals who are codependent battle with what their identity is and what their motivation is. Once in a while, they are mindful and sensitive to their internal identity talk, and every now and then, have no clue what they like or do not care for.

Limit building: One of the most significant strides to ace in the voyage of codependency recuperation is figuring out how to construct proper enthusiastic limits. Helping the individual with codependency in discovering that the person in question doesn't have control over others is a critical advance in creating solid connections.

Learning self-approval: People with codependency regularly have a dubious meaning of self, so directing an individual to figure out how to endure awkward sentiments, let go of pointless examples of conduct, and practice self-approval will help during the time spent structure confidence.

Codependency has been alluded to as "relationship addiction" or "love addiction." The emphasis on others lightens our torment and internal void, however, in disregarding ourselves, it just develops. This propensity turns into a round, self-sustaining framework that takes on its very own life. Our reasoning winds up over the top, and our conduct can be habitual, notwithstanding unfavorable outcomes. Models may call an partner or ex we realize we shouldn't, putting ourselves or qualities in danger to suit somebody, or snooping out of desire or dread. This is the reason codependency has been alluded to as an addiction. In 1956, it chose that addiction was a sickness, and in 2013, additionally named heftiness a malady. A prime inspiration in the two cases was to de-deride these conditions and empower treatment.

Is Codependency a Disease?

In 1988, therapists recommended that codependency is an illness taking note of the addictive procedure. A therapist and specialist of interior medication, Charles Whitfield, portrayed codependence as an interminable and dynamic ailment of "lost-selfhood" with unmistakable, treatable side effects — simply like substance reliance.

Codependency is additionally portrayed by manifestations that shift on a continuum like those related to chronic drug use. They go from gentle to serious and incorporate reliance, forswearing, dysfunctional passionate reactions, longing for and remunerate (through connection with someone else), and failure to control or swear off urgent conduct without treatment. You progressively invest energy contemplating, being with, and additionally attempting to control someone else, similarly as a medication junkie with a medication. Other social, recreational, or work exercises endure accordingly. At long last, you may proceed with your conduct as well as the relationship, in spite of relentless or repeating social or relational issues it makes.

Phases of Codependency

Codependency is constant with suffering side effects that are additionally dynamic, implying that they intensify after some time without intercession and treatment. As I would see it, codependency starts in youth because of a dysfunctional family condition. In any case, youngsters are normally reliant; it cannot be analyzed until adulthood, and for the most part, starts to manifest in cozy connections. There are three identifiable stages prompting expanding reliance on the individual or relationship and comparing loss of self-center and self-care.

Beginning period

The beginning period may resemble any sentimental association with expanded consideration and reliance on your partner and want to satisfy the person in question. Be that as it may, with codependency, we can wind up fixated on the individual, deny or defend risky conduct, question our discernments, neglect to keep up sound limits and surrender our own companions and exercises.

Center Stage

Bit by bit, there is expanded exertion required to limit excruciating parts of the relationship, and uneasiness, blame, and self-accuse set in. After some time, our confidence decreases as we bargain a greater amount of ourselves to keep up the relationship. Outrage, dissatisfaction, and hatred develop. Then we empower or attempt to change our partner through consistence, control, annoying, or accusing. We may conceal issues and pull back from family and companions. There might possibly be misuse or brutality, however, our state of mind declines, and fixation, reliance, and struggle, withdrawal, or consistence increases. We may utilize other addictive practices to adapt, for example, eating less junk food, shopping, working, or mishandling substances.

Late Stage

Presently, the enthusiastic and social side effects start to influence our wellbeing. We may experience pressure-related issues, for example, stomach related and rest issues, migraines, muscle strain or agony, dietary issues, TMJ, sensitivities, sciatica, and coronary illness. Over the top impulsive conduct or different addictions increment, just as the absence of confidence and self-care. Sentiments of sadness, outrage, gloom, and misery develop.

Recuperation

Fortunately, the indications are reversible when a codependent enters treatment. Individuals do not look for assistance until there is an emergency or they're in enough agony to persuade them. Ordinarily, they aren't mindful of their codependency and may likewise be willfully ignorant about another person's maltreatment as well as addiction. Recovery starts with instruction and leaving refusal. Finding out about codependency is a decent start, yet more prominent change happens through treatment and going to a Twelve-Step program.

In recuperation, you increase trust and the center shifts from the other individual to yourself. There are early, middle, and late phases of recuperation that parallel recuperation from different addictions. In the center stage, you start to manufacture your very own character, confidence, and the capacity to decisively express sentiments, needs, and needs. You learn self-obligation, limits, and self-care. Psychotherapy frequently incorporates mending PTSD and youth injury.

In the late stage, joy and confidence don't rely upon others. You gain the limit with regard to both self-sufficiency and closeness. You experience your own capacity and self-esteem. You feel broad and innovative, with the capacity to produce and seek after your own objectives.

Codependency doesn't consequently vanish when an individual leaves a codependent relationship. Recuperation requires progressing support, and there is no ideal restraint. In any case, codependent conduct can, without much of a stretch, return under expanded pressure or if you go into a dysfunctional relationship. Hairsplitting is a side effect of codependency. There is nothing of the sort as immaculate recuperation. Repeating side effects simply present continuous learning openings.

Abuse

Connections between individuals are solid when they are interconnected. In an interconnected relationship, every individual has their very own needs addressed and endeavors to address the issues of the other individual. An issue happens, nonetheless, when connections are interconnected, yet are codependent.

In codependent connections, the requirements of one individual being filled by the other are undesirable or improper. One of the most well-known situations of codependency is a heavy drinker who is routinely provided with alcohol by the other individual in the relationship, despite the fact that the alcoholic can turn out to be verbally or physically oppressive when inebriated. The inquiry at that point moves toward becoming, "For what reason would that individual oblige and even help such conduct?" The appropriate response is codependency, and frequently, the reason is psychological mistreatment.

The genuinely manhandled end up in codependent connections in light of a craving to be required, regardless of whether the need is to give the following beverage. Also, despite the fact that a relationship is codependent, in any event, it is needy in some sense. Psychological mistreatment frequently scars the victim. They feel dishonorable to be adored, all by themselves. In a codependent relationship, their value is effectively characterized. They are regularly advised that they are so critical to that individual, particularly when they are giving what that individual needs. To feel esteem, even dependent on unseemly or destructive conduct, the individual who has been genuinely manhandled will go into or proceed in an unfortunate codependent relationship.

The psychological mistreatment succeeds when the abuser can supplant your own authority over yourself with their control. You never again confide in yourself, yet rather enable the abuser to hold undue impact over your considerations and activities. The abuser progresses toward becoming, generally, a piece of you, controlling you and how you see yourself and your reality. The limit between where you start and the abuser closures is obscured.

In resulting connections, you may end up totally surrendering to the next individual, thoroughly submerging yourself in the other individual's character, tolerating their perspective on the world and of you. Lamentably, you may look for somebody who is predominant and controlling with whom to set up a relationship. The jobs in this new relationship will fit into an anticipated example.

Then again, you might be incredibly touchy to anything you think appears to be remotely similar to control. It might be difficult for you to keep up cozy connections, on the grounds that to have closeness may trigger an exceptionally delicate reaction on your part. Also, you might be exceptionally suspicious of any individual who tries to become acquainted with you in a profound, individual manner. You may set up boundaries to keep individuals out.

At long last, there is simply the peril of ending up very retained. If your experience has consistently been that whatever you did or didn't do brought a quick, extraordinary response, you may have reasoned that the world truly did, in actuality, spin around you. You may have built up a propensity for dissecting everything that occurs around you as it identifies with you.

While these strategies helped you endure your maltreatment, they have left you not well arranged to work inside solid, positive connections. Endeavoring to submerge yourself totally into a solid relationship may make you seem possessive and tenacious or choking to the next individual. Then again, a doubt of closeness and a general standoffish quality may prevent most others from endeavoring an association with you. What's more, being amazingly self-retained practically rules out contemplations of others.

If you do not have a clue what a codependent relationship is, it is when two individuals in a relationship give up their freedom and build up an undesirable reliance on one another. In this, one partner is so fixated on the requirements of the other that they overlook their very own needs. Therefore, the other partner controls the relationship in an egotistical and regularly injurious way.

This is a perilous dynamic, yet it is not as simple to identify as you may suspect. While codependent connections may have physical maltreatment, all have enthusiastic and mental maltreatment. This kind of maltreatment is regularly very difficult to identify. It gradually crawls into the relationship and turns into an example of conduct that the codependent cannot change.

The causes of psychological mistreatment in a relationship can begin all of a sudden, or they can build slowly. Regularly, what's seen by the codependent partner as cherishing and mindful partner is really a controller, a stalker, and an individual who is separating and nourishing off the requirements of the codependent.

The Effects and Impact of Emotional, Mental, and Verbal Abuse

The different traits we all have affect the people around us in different ways an it is important to understand the impact they have on relationships.

Since codependents dread being separated from everyone else and get such a large amount of their identity from their association with their partner, they have issues saying no or defending themselves when they start to experience misuse. Saying no frequently brings about progressively verbal maltreatment, seclusion, and dangers to leave—all issues that are actually what the codependent is attempting to keep away from.

This creates a situation where the narcisstic iniviual takes avantage of the one who is codependent and they are unable to do without each other.

It is critical to understand that, much the same as physical maltreatment, the enthusiastic, mental, and verbal maltreatment is purposeful behavior by the abuser. The narcissist utilizes this conduct to get what they need, purposefully tearing down the other individual's confidence, self-esteem, and capacity to support themselves.

Perceiving Gaslighting

Another regular type of passionate and verbal maltreatment is gaslighting. This is definitely not another conduct, however it is as of late been identified and named as a conduct utilized by the individuals who take part in psychological mistreatment.

Gaslighting is, here and there, more difficult to distinguish and more harming than some different sorts of psychological mistreatment. In this kind of maltreatment, the abuser controls the codependent by giving false data or false memories that reason the codependent to start to scrutinize their rational soundness and their capacity to review and recall things effectively.

At times, gaslighting is the utilization of refusals that things happened. This is not just differences in memory. It is malignant, purposeful, and intended to make blame, vulnerability, and uncertainty in your brain.

There are some regular signs that gaslighting is going on the relationship. To help identify this conduct, search for the accompanying:

Giving false data: To justify a lie, an abuser giving false information will discuss other individuals. For instance, a man may tell a lady she was playing with somebody at a gathering, and everybody saw and was discussing it. He may make articulations about what others said and how they saw the conduct.

Concealing conduct: If an partner is trapped in a falsehood, frequently they will utilize misleads endeavor to clarify away the issue. In any case, the untruths are rehashed again and again, and might be clearly incorrect records of what has happened. Simultaneously, the codependent is probably not going to challenge the untruth, and it continues getting rehashed until it is hard for the codependent to review the specifics of the circumstance.

As gaslighting can be difficult to recognize, conversing with an advisor and building a solid encouraging group of people will be basic to evade further harm to your confidence.

Illnesses

One of the most testing parts of life is shaping sound bonds and associations with others. Frequently now and again, an individual who has encountered injury shapes an undesirable faithfulness to others. This implies that the unfortunate casualties have a specific dysfunctional connections that happen within the sight of peril, disgrace, or misuse.

In these connections, an individual may encounter more mishandle, self-damage, fixation, doubt, and other negative outcomes of the bond. Another, and normal, aftereffect of addiction and harsh conditions, is codependency. Codependency alludes to a kind of dysfunctional relationship where one individual empowers someone else's addiction, poor emotional well-being, adolescence, untrustworthiness, or under-accomplishment.

Co-dependency can be a difficult issue to work with in treatment since it can turn into an unrecognizable addiction. Frequently, one winds up over the top with the relationship and bond they shaped with another that it is regularly not seen that their bond is undesirable. An individual cannot control their bond with someone else paying little heed to the treachery, decimation, or misuse. The individual who has co-dependency problem is increasingly centered around the abuser. So as to mend and discover injury goals, an individual must be capable and willing to perceive how their habitual conduct just guides in shaping injury bonds and in this way they should break the compulsivity.

Codependency then again, concentrates more on the addiction. Injury holding and codependency possibly meet up when the someone who is addicted is likewise an oppressive culprit. The individual who will in general be codependent likely was engaged with some type of addiction through relatives, companions, and so on. Along these lines, the individual is activated by other people who have addiction. Codependency is additionally not "terrifying" yet increasingly about thinking about others needs rather than their own. In treating codependency, it is significant for the individual to be increasingly mindful of one's self, reasonability, and permitting care into their lives from themselves.

In treating others, it is essential to perceive the difference between injury holding and codependency. Shaping relationship are difficult in their very own right, yet when including injury, treachery, stress, addiction, misuse, and absence of self-care, connections can turn out to be very unfortunate and there is a requirement for intercessions. Both injury holding and codependency can cause extreme outcomes. It is imperative to enable the individual to identify whether a relationship has turned out to be addictive or whether they should disengage affectionately and care for themselves. Frequently this can be accomplished by dismembering associations with a specialist and figuring out how to define fitting limits and give up. Since with the give up and acknowledgment of how to break the undesirable bonds, an individual builds up their actual feeling of self and capacity to make dependable and solid connections.

"In a war, warriors are compelled to deny their feelings so as to endure. This enthusiastic disavowal attempts to enable the warrior to endure the war, yet later can have obliterating postponed results. The restorative calling has now perceived the injury and harm that this enthusiastic refusal can cause, and have instituted a term to depict the impacts of this sort of forswearing. That term is "Postponed Stress Syndrome."

In a war fighters need to deny what it feels like to see companions executed and debilitated; what it feels like to murder other individuals and make them endeavor to slaughter you. There is injury brought about by the occasions themselves. There is injury because of the need of preventing the enthusiastic effect from claiming the occasions. There is injury from the impacts the passionate refusal has on the individual's life after he/she has come back from the war in light of the fact that as long is the individual is denying his/her enthusiastic injury she/he is precluding a section from claiming her/himself.

The pressure brought about by the injury, and the impact of denying the injury, by denying self, in the end surfaces in manners which produce new injury - nervousness, liquor and medication misuse, bad dreams, wild rage, failure to look after connections, powerlessness to hold employments, suicide, and so forth.

Codependence is a type of Delayed Stress Syndrome.

Rather than blood and demise (albeit some experience blood and passing actually), what befell us as youngsters was otherworldly demise and enthusiastic harming, mental torment and physical infringement. We had to grow up preventing the truth from securing what was going on in our homes. We had to deny our sentiments about what we were encountering and seeing and detecting. We had to deny ourselves.

We grew up denying the enthusiastic reality: of parental liquor abuse, addiction, dysfunctional behavior, rage, viciousness, misery, surrender, double-crossing, hardship, disregard, inbreeding, and so on and so on.; of our folks battling or the fundamental pressure and outrage since they weren't being straightforward enough to battle; of father's overlooking us due to his workaholism as well as mother covering us since she had no other personality than being a mother; of the maltreatment that one parent stacked on another who wouldn't safeguard him/herself and additionally the maltreatment we got from one of our folks while the other wouldn't shield us; of having just one parent or of having two guardians who remained together and shouldn't have; and so forth., and so forth.

We grew up with messages like: kids ought to be seen and not heard; huge young men do not cry and little women do not blow up; it is not alright to resent somebody you adore - particularly your folks; god cherishes you however will send you to consume in hellfire always if you contact your dishonorable private parts; do not make commotion or run or in any capacity be a typical youngster; do not commit errors or do anything incorrectly; and so on., and so forth.

We were naturally introduced to the center of a war where our feeling of self was battered and cracked and broken into pieces. We experienced childhood in war zones where our creatures were limited, our discernments refuted, and our sentiments overlooked and nullified.

The war we were naturally introduced to, the front line every one of us experienced childhood in, was not in some outside nation against some identified "foe" - it was in the "homes" which should be our place of refuge with our folks whom we Loved and trusted to deal with us. It was not for a year or a few - it was for sixteen or seventeen or eighteen years.

We encountered what is classified "asylum injury" - our most secure spot to be was not protected - and we encountered it once a day for quite a long time and years. The absolute most noteworthy harm was done to us in inconspicuous ways regularly on the grounds that our haven was a war zone.

It was anything but a front line in light of the fact that our folks weren't right or awful - it was a war zone since they were at war inside, on the grounds that they were naturally introduced to the center of a war. By doing our mending we are turning into the sincerely legit good examples that our folks never got the opportunity to be. Through being in Recovery we are breaking the cycles of foolish conduct that have managed human presence for a huge number of years.

Codependence is an awful and amazing type of Delayed Stress Syndrome. The injury of feeling like we were not protected in our very own homes makes it exceptionally difficult to feel like we are sheltered anyplace. Having an inclination that we were not adorable to our very own folks makes it difficult to accept that anybody can Love us.

Codependence is being at war with ourselves - which makes it difficult to trust and Love ourselves. Codependence is precluding parts from claiming ourselves so we do not have the foggiest idea what our identity is.

Recuperation from the malady of Codependence includes halting the war inside so we can connect with our True Self, so we can begin to Love and confide in ourselves."

Chapter 3 – The Recovery Process

Setting Boundaries

In sentimental connections we frequently consider limits an awful thing or basically superfluous. Is not our partner expected to foresee our needs and needs? Is not that piece of being infatuated? Aren't limits unfeeling? Do not they meddle with the sentiment and immediacy of a relationship?

Every solid relationship have limits. A limit is "where I end and another person starts." Boundaries seeing someone are compared to the limits around states.

With no line the differentiation ends up confounding: Who possesses and keeps up this questionable space? Which guidelines apply?

At the point when the limit is obviously characterized and regarded, you needn't bother with dividers or electric wall, he said. Individuals can even cross the limit every so often when there is a shared comprehension. Be that as it may, when the limit is damaged so as to do mischief or exploit, at that point you'll likely need dividers, doors and watchmen.

In sound connections partners ask consent, consider each other's emotions, show appreciation and regard differences in conclusion, point of view and sentiments.

In less sound connections, partners expect their partner feels a similar way they do. They overlook the impacts of disregarding their partner's limit (e.g., "They'll get over it").

Limits in sentimental connections are particularly basic, on the grounds that instead of different connections, partners possess each other's most private spaces, including physical, enthusiastic and sexual, he said.

This is the reason imparting your limits obviously is vital. Be that as it may, what does — and doesn't — this resemble?

Beneath, you'll discover bits of knowledge on limits that do not work and tips for defining limits that do.

Limits that Do not Work

Limits that frequently fizzle are those that incorporate the words 'consistently,' 'never' or any supreme language. Such limits are normally unreasonable and do not last.

Other poor limits estrange you from your partner, have a twofold standard or attempt to control a result. If you aren't home by 8 p.m. consistently, I will not engage in sexual relations with you," "If you do not do X, I will hurt myself" or "You are not permitted to do X, yet I can do it when I please."

Obscure limits additionally do not work. These incorporate "Do not spend a great deal of cash this month" or "Get the children from school a couple of times each week."

Numerous partners do not discuss their limits. They anticipate that their partner should simply know them. This is out of line. For example, you need your partner to perceive your achievements. Rather than communicating this need, you indicate it, play a round of "I'll luxuriously confirm you if you'll furnish a proportional payback" or sulk around when it doesn't occur.

In addition to the fact that this is incapable, it makes disarray and can hurt your relationship.

Defining Healthy Limits

As per analyst Leslie Becker-Phelps, Ph.D, sound limits incorporate everything from making some noise when you believe you are being disregarded to supporting for yourself to possess energy for your own advantages.

Attempt the sandwich approach. This comprises of a compliment, analysis, compliment. Beginning with a compliment keeps your partner from getting protective. "This primes them for a little analysis, they feel associated and agreeable enough to take it, and after that it closes with a compliment."

Model: "I cherish engaging in sexual relations with you, it is a mind blowing some portion of our relationship. I find that I'm for the most part in the state of mind in the first part of the prior day work, and around evening time I simply need to rest. Would we be able to continue having the best sex ever in the mornings?"

Be clear about your needs. After you realize what your needs are, tell your partner. Numerous limit infringement come from errors. One partner has an issue with specific practices, yet they never let their partner know. Regularly this is on the grounds that they stress it'll trigger a contention.

Be that as it may, it is OK to have inclinations, and it is OK to tell your darling. For example, if you need to be treated as an equivalent with budgetary issues, tell your partner.

Be specific and direct. As indicated by Levy, the more specific you are with imparting your limit, the better. She shared these models:

"If you put your messy garments in the hamper by 10 a.m. on Saturday morning, I'll be glad to wash them for you."

"Try not to peruse my diary. I feel damaged when my security is slighted."

"I need to catch wind of your day. I'll be accessible to give you my complete consideration in 10 minutes."

Be clear about your adoration, while being clear about your limits. Convey to your partner the amount you care about them. If they've exceeded a limit, notice this. "State that you need them to regard the limit, and clarify the significance of this to you."

"I cherish you however am not willing to phone in wiped out for you when you have been drinking."

She shared this model: "I need you to realize that I cherish you and have each goal of us working through whatever issues come up. In any case, I disapprove of you being verbally harsh when you blow up. If you need to discuss how it upset you that I kept running into my former sweetheart, we can do that, yet just if you do not assault me."

Becker-Phelps additionally recommended staying open to hearing how the limit influences your partner. Talk through the issue so both of you feel regarded, heard and thought about, she said.

Use "I" proclamations. As per Levy, "I" explanations "help you claim your own sentiments and enable your partner to feel more quiet and less protective." Rather than saying, "You have to do this," or "You ought to consistently," utilize such expresses as: "I feel," or "I would acknowledge," or "I might want it if... "

Act naturally mindful. The initial phase in defining any limit is self-information. You have to recognize what you like and aversion, what you are OK with versus what panics you, and how you need to be treated in given circumstances.

While there is no assurance this will consistently work, individuals will in general be progressively responsive to analysis when they first feel heard and comprehended.

At last, sound connections require obvious parameters. For example, most couples concur that deceiving is a limit infringement. Yet, I do not get cheating's meaning? Is it physical contact, going to lunch, imparting insider facts to a partner, fantasizing about somebody or watching pornography?

At the point when couples are clear about the limits for their own relationship, what the principles, objectives, and desires are, the relationship can be steady.

Putting Yourself First

Self-Care

Declining to deal with yourself doesn't make you a saint deserving of awards yet rather presumably an all out torment to live with. This may sound nonsensical however bodes well if you think about that we as a whole need the ones we want to be glad, solid, and around for whatever length of time that conceivable. You may stress your partner by not dealing with your wellbeing since this may mean losing you to a preventable ailment.

Comparative principles apply when you do not deal with your enthusiastic wellbeing. Perhaps you are discouraged or constantly troubled at work yet will not change employments or get help through treatment. You may feel qualified for your partner's compassion consistently and that is consistent with some degree. Life can be tireless and periodically gives us a crude arrangement yet when your misery ends up incessant and you stay aloof about fixing the issue, requesting proceeded with compassion transforms into a childish demonstration. No one needs to return home to wretchedness consistently.

Besides, it is extremely excruciating to see our friends and family endure so you are by all account not the only one in torment when you are troubled. In truth, none of us can provide for others what we cannot provide for ourselves so our ability to deal with ourselves and satisfy ourselves is firmly attached to our capacity to provide for others liberally. Both of you merit a significant other who assumes liability for their wellbeing and satisfaction.

In this way, despite the fact that you may feel pulled in various ways by the entirety of your obligations, set aside a few minutes consistently for these fundamental strides of self-care:

Look for approaches to develop and figure out how to remain occupied with life.

This could be perusing another creator or building up another diversion. When we are youthful, everything provokes our interest and feels new and energizing yet as we get more seasoned, it is anything but difficult to simply stay with a similar old, same old. Try not to exhaust and unsurprising however rather observe something new to be energized and converse with your partner about.

Eat well, get enough rest, and exercise routinely.

Life is short and you just get one body to live it with so treat it like the essential need it is. Utilize sound judgment and deal with it consistently in little ways and enormous.

Invest quality energy as a team.

Shut occasions out each week where you do not participate in pressure talk about work, bills, and so on. Rather, see a motion picture together or plan an excursion to the recreation center or exhibition hall. During those occasions, turn off your PDA. Regardless of whether it is a full night out or simply making up for lost time in the first part of the day or night, having even only 30 minutes of together time can help with fashioning a more grounded bond. Feeling near others is nature's Prozac without the expenses and symptoms so use it liberally.

Invest energy with loved ones.

We are social creatures and nothing feeds us like our connections. Offering a chuckle to friends and family makes our ordinary stresses fall away and interfaces us to something greater. This experience is pivotal for our prosperity since it assuages pressure.

Dealing with yourself physically and genuinely makes you progressively present, centered, and quiet. Be the individual that you would need to get back home to, somebody who chips away at their own prosperity and satisfaction and hence has the transmission capacity to make another person cheerful as well.

To wrap things up, if you feel that your partner is not rehearsing self-care, make some noise and converse with them about it. Call attention to why it makes a difference to you and how it influences your relationship. Be strong and energetic about it as much as you can and offer recommendations. Ideally, your partner will be available to your endeavors to improve the nature of the relationship. If the individual in question is not, you can generally attempt couple's treatment to improve correspondence.

Mindfulness and Meditation

Care is a frame of mind to living that encourages you be progressively open, caring, and mindful. It includes purposely coordinating your consideration away from autopilot and negative, making a decision about musings, enabling you to be progressively present and associated with whatever is going on this moment. It is anything but a major stretch to envision that increasingly careful individuals may improve relationship partners. Furthermore, presently there is clear research support for this relationship. A meta-investigation distributed in the Journal of Human Sciences and Extension a year ago found that more elevated amounts of care anticipate more joyful, all the more fulfilling connections.

Does care really cause relationship upgrades?

Before we go any further, it is critical to take note of that of the 10 investigations that were incorporated, just two contained a care mediation. The others simply estimated care and relationship fulfillment and found a positive connection between them (correlational investigations). This raises the chicken and egg issue. Do more joyful connections make us feel increasingly present and open, as opposed to the a different way? In spite of the fact that we do not know without a doubt that care produces relationship improvement, in any event two investigations demonstrate that it does. In any case, why? The appropriate response may lie in how care influences the cerebrum.

The following are five cerebrum based manners by which rehearsing care may enable you to have more joyful connections:

1. Care improves feeling guideline

Studies demonstrate that care practice fortifies the prefrontal cortex and improves the availability between the prefrontal cortex and amygdala. The prefrontal cortex is the cerebrum's official focus and it can make an impression on the amygdala revealing to it that things are alright and it can chill and stop the "battle, flight, solidify" reaction. So notwithstanding when we do begin to lose it or leave our partners when they are highly involved with talking, we can say "Stop! This is not useful" and in this way prevent ourselves from going down a relationship bunny opening.

2. Care encourages us be progressively present and mindful

The vast majority of us realize how disappointing it tends to be to attempt to converse with an partner who is continually checking email or messages or whose consideration is consistently on work stresses. Care changes territories of the cerebrum related with coordinating consideration and core interest. In this manner, care can enable us to see when we are on autopilot and divert thoughtfulness regarding whatever our partner is stating or to what they might feel and requiring. This can enable us to be additionally cherishing and present in our connections, which assembles closeness and makes our connections more joyful and progressively associated.

3. Care makes us increasingly empathic

Care additionally changes the insula, a piece of the mind related with sympathy and empathy. This can enable us to be all the more comprehension of our partners' viewpoints and feelings and feel more sympathy for them. When we approach our partners sympathetically, as opposed to with resentment and want to control them, this can take the discussion a positive way. Sympathy additionally encourages us express love and warmth to our partner, which manufactures closeness. Care makes a methodology, as opposed to an evasion attitude.

4. Care upgrades mindfulness

Care likewise prompts changes in the foremost cingulate cortex, which is related with our feeling of self and feeling guideline. In this way care may enable us to see when we are carrying on in undesirable ways and divert consideration back to how we'd like to act and what our guiding principle are. This can enable us to control the motivation to act dangerously or manipulatively. It might enable you to get up and accomplish something different when you are enticed to break into your partner's PC or stalk them on the web.

5. Care brings down negative enthusiastic reactivity

Care studies demonstrate that rehearsing care for 8 to 10 weeks changes the cerebrum's feeling guideline regions. The amygdala is a little, almond-molded piece of the midbrain that captures the cerebrum into "battle, flight, solidify" mode in which we begin to consider our to be as dangers to our prosperity or self-sufficiency and naturally shut down sincerely or begin to assault them with furious words and deeds. Care contracts the volume of the amygdala, implying that it has less capacity to capture us into 'danger" mode. This can help couples escape negative cycles of damaging contending or passionate removing.

We as a whole need more joyful connections however few of us know the keys to relationship fulfillment. Instead of concentrating vitality on grumbling or attempting to change your partner, take up a care practice. Far and away superior, take a care course together or practice reflection utilizing a care application. This will enable you to be progressively present, cherishing, and sincerely develop. What's more, who can oppose that?

Let Your Emotions Out

Peculiar things happen when we get injured. Hurt is a tragic inclination; subsequently, it bodes well that we would react in misery when a life partner or relative (irregular models, I guarantee you) offends us. Be that as it may, rather than crying about our torment in such cases, we are undeniably bound to lash out in fierceness! Go figure.

Things being what they are, our response is reasonable. Outrage has two variations: essential displeasure and optional indignation. Essential annoyance happens when a limit has been crossed. Infringement sign fury as a safeguard system so as to prepare a viable reaction. For example, if we happen to observe Anger has two variations; a harasser strolling by our sweet young lady and pulls hard on her hair, our moment fury will enable us to make fast move to address the circumstance. Something very similar happens when our own limits are disregarded in child rearing: Picture a youngster not tuning in to his parent. Everything inside the parent says this situation is not right, and fury regularly ascends to the surface ("you have to tune in to your folks, youthful man!"). In this circumstance, be that as it may, we have to kill the annoyance flag and chill off a piece so as to think of the best and suitable child rearing arrangement.

Optional annoyance—brutal as it in some cases may be—is, at its center, a passionate injury instead of a sign. Here and there called "receptive outrage," it is an enthusiastic reaction as opposed to an unadulterated feeling. The unadulterated feeling is harmed. At the point when an individual feels hurt, the person may react with indignation. It is actually the same than if the individual reacted by hitting the sack. In the previous case (when an individual gets distraught), the reaction is enthusiastic in nature; in the last case (when the individual hits the hay), the reaction is social in nature.

In the two cases, the genuine inclination being experienced is harmed.

We should picture a spouse saying something harmful to his wife (once more, you may need to consider something you read some place . . .). When the words leave his mouth, she feels a cut in her heart. It is instinctive. It harms.

Wife: "I have a good thought! For what reason do not we take a family excursion? The children would love it!"

Spouse: "Do you ever think before you open your mouth?"

Presently, I realize you may ask why the spouse would state a wonder such as this, yet remember marriage is perplexing, and couple of things are what they appear from the start to be. For this situation, for example, this couple has been talking about the spouse's agonizing money related worry for half a month in their conjugal directing. He has communicated his dread of getting a cardiovascular failure from all the weight he feels. With the instructor's assistance, they have gone to an understanding that the wife will, throughout the following couple of months, abstain from requesting that the spouse burn through cash on any "additional items" for the family. Without It is instinctive. It harms. Thinking, be that as it may, the wife currently energetically raises the possibility of a family excursion, which will of need include some cost. Subsequently the spouse's burning answer.

Her very own conduct in any case, the wife reels in torment. "How might he converse with me like that?" she ponders. She feels rejected, squashed, abused and extremely, hurt. So she opens her mouth and starts screaming at her better half. "How could YOU SPEAK TO ME LIKE THAT? DO YOU EVER THINK BEFORE OPENING

YOUR MOUTH? YOU ARE MEAN, DISGUSTING, DESPICABLE . . ."
That is optional outrage.

Our sages disclose to us that outrage is a hazardous inclination. Outrage can cause enormous profound mischief, just as passionate, mental and physical damage. It prompts numerous wrongdoings, including the offenses of harming individuals with words, treating individuals forcefully, utilizing foul language, and numerous others. Optional annoyance is the most perilous sort of all since, sitting as it does on an open injury, one is probably going to lash out with the full power of the enthusiastic agony that releases it. Words once verbally expressed cannot be withdrawn. Who knows what number of broken relationships are the aftereffect of hearts broken by reactionary verbal maltreatment?

So as to maintain a strategic distance from the statement of reactionary resentment, we should prepare ourselves to keep our mouths solidly shut at whatever point we feels aches of hurt. It offers a reward "more brilliant than the sun" to the individuals who can ace this aptitude. That reward will occur on the planet to come, however there are additionally remunerates that happen directly here, in this world. With our mouths shut, our talking device cannot turn into an instrument of the underhanded tendency. We are spared from profound mischief. Also, our most significant connections are spared from annihilation. We can relieve ourselves, quiet down and investigate the circumstance all the more rapidly in light of the fact that we have not expanded the science of wrath. We can start to see the blunders of our own specific manners, picking up, developing and improving therefore. We are additionally ready to think and make sense of what steps should be taken so as to rectify the circumstance. It is everything great!

So as to turn into an ace of discretion, practice We can alleviate ourselves; keeping your mouth shut in minor, ordinary episodes when you need to "answer back," counter or have the final word. As you show signs of improvement and better at this expertise, you will wind up prepared to deal with greater difficulties, until at last you will have the option to keep your mouth shut in the exact instant you are injured, regardless of how harmed you feel. And after that you will satisfy the expressions of Proverbs: "Who is a tough individual? One who has restraint!"

Redefining Perspectives

Aren't connections only a breeze! Said nobody, ever. Let's be honest, we are intricate animals and when we work together with another mind boggling animal we can deliver a rainbow of bright and disorganized outcomes. Getting to the meaningful part of unwinding that coupledom is no simple procedure and the last snap, well it constantly will in general leave an imprint. Our life can truly feel like the crude skin abandoned after the savage ripping off of a mortar — we as a whole know the sensation.

What however, after the tempest of parting has settled? Amidst connections, we bond, we mate and in some cases we even make (other little people) thus as we go separate ways, what of those subtleties? Huge or little, the things we do together all exude with vitality and a mental and once in a while physical result (kids, home... things). Isolating our time and our things to provide food for the reminisce of a relationship is the most exceedingly awful sort of maths on the planet... Who gets what and when? It is regularly difficult and constantly precarious.

The thing with us people is that we will in general place a colossal measure of significance on our connections; we endeavor to mate for life and we always remember we have loved ones, regardless of how it 'so occurred'. The issue is, a lot of connections do not length the eternity course of events and between the underlying tornado of profoundly charged feeling and the unfolding of the real world; offering your life to someone else is truly bleeding hard. The thing is, when love blurs and connections separate, we have options, we can pick how to respond and even proceed to make companionships from the most fierce and sharp of partitions. It is difficult, however it is so advantageous and if there are kids amidst a separation, at that point it is everything the more imperative to pick a co-child rearing game plan that breeds regard and reasonableness; no tyke has the right to be stuck in the middle of two warring grown-ups.

Connections arrive at an end for a wide range of reasons and a portion of those reasons can be forcefully terrible; disloyalty is a noteworthy player with respect to reasons for separation and no uncertainty, finding a kinship borne from such a circumstance is now and again incomprehensible. If you do not have youngsters then there is no genuine should be companions with a miscreant, yet if you do have children... Well, it is a hard trudge, yet it is possible and advantageous; to make something that shields your kids from the drop out of a split. Pardoning is one of the hardest yet most compensating things and if it implies harmony for your family, at that point it is the best approach to push ahead.

Discovering some shared view makes for a decent start when moving toward another point of view on connections. Where there was once love, there are recollections and those mean something when you attempt to find out a companionship subsequent to parting. Concentrating on the great and the positive can open up a universe of chances to be companions with an ex and really, the commonality without the sex or closeness has been known to make lifelong kinships. Rethinking your association with somebody you once adored needn't be an errand or a weight.

Anyway, how would we approach rethinking a relationship? Three Cs...

Thought — having sympathy truly encourages us to interface. We probably will not comprehend or even concur with somebody's activities or point of view, yet attempting to stroll from their perspective for a moment is an absolute necessity in pushing ahead.

Correspondence — numerous couples quit conveying during their relationship and it is simply after that they can reconnect and really hear each out other.

Bargain — compromising with some place with regards to reconnecting with an ex makes for a marginally less crabby beginning. There is an incredible saying in such manner, "Do not anticipate even more a man (or lady) than he (or she) is ready or ready to give." Keeping desires reasonable and being transparent with an ex can ingrain trust and regard just as setting up limits so everybody knows where they stand.

As far as evidence, I am it. My ex and I are currently great companions and bringing up our little girl together while we're not together is ending up being loaded with happiness. Making it to the Nativity together, putting on a splendid birthday end of the week for her and being there as a group for her is our sole need however the advantages of hanging out and having a snicker are certainly a reward as well. In a New York Times Modern Love section titled "Joyfully Ever, After We Split," Wendy Paris subtleties the advancement of her association with her better half through the separation procedure and how isolating united them.

Gwynny and Chris from Coldplay went separate ways with their popular articulation, 'cognizant uncoupling' which, at the time appeared to be fairly dubious (and sounded a bit self important) however in all actuality, it is actually what's going on.

Uncoupling with beauty and pushing ahead as companions... The present day, 'cheerfully ever after.'

Listen to Others

Generally, in all connections there is one individual who talks and one who tunes in. Be that as it may, is the audience truly tuning in?.

The objective of profound listening is to get data, comprehend an individual or a circumstance, and experience delight. Undivided attention is tied in with settling on a cognizant choice to hear what individuals are stating. It is tied in with being totally centered around others—their words and their messages—without being occupied.

It is been said that one of the most widely recognized reasons why individuals see advisors is to have their accounts heard. So as to have your story heard, you need an audience. Tuning in and sympathy abilities are the signs of good communicators, pioneers, and advisors. Listening aptitudes can be adapted, however actually, a few people simply will in general be preferred audience members over others.

The significance of tuning in relational connections cannot be overemphasized. One examination demonstrated that there are two different kinds of tuning in: "tuning in to comprehend" and "tuning in to react." Those who "tune in to comprehend" have more prominent fulfillment in their relational connections than others. While individuals may figure they may tune in to comprehend, what they're truly doing is holding on to react.

Furthermore, when people attempt to "fix" other individuals, they are frequently reacting to their very own need to impact. A similar report demonstrated that couples who have experienced treatment together are better listeners because they can directly apply advice to their relationships. It is been said that ladies as a rule need to be heard, and men need to fix or react.

As indicated by clinicians, dynamic or profound listening is at the core of each sound relationship. It is additionally the best method to realize development and change. The individuals who are heard will in general be increasingly open, progressively majority rule in their ways, and are regularly less guarded. Great audience members cease from making decisions, and give a sheltered domain and holder for speakers.

By listening cautiously when somebody talks, we're revealing to them that we care about what they're stating. It is additionally imperative to recollect that listening is infectious. When we tune in to other people, at that point chances are they will be progressively disposed to hear us out.

Fortunately we can figure out how to be better audience members; notwithstanding, listening takes practice. The more we do it, the better we get at it, and the more constructive our relational connections will be.

Here are a few hints for improving as an audience:

Notice the speaker's tone and enunciation.

Develop sympathy.

Abstain from making decisions.

Rehash in your very own words what somebody has let you know (compassionate reflection).

Recognize that you are tuning in by gesturing or saying "Uh-huh."

Put yourself inside the brain of the speaker.

Focus on non-verbal communication.

Investigate others' eyes when they're talking.

Focus on the sentiments related with the words.

Once in a while outline others' remarks when given the opportunity.

Tune in for importance.

To turn into a compelling communicator, you have to figure out how to listen the same amount of as you have to figure out how to talk. Shockingly, a great many people center more around the talking than they do on the tuning in. Regardless of whether in a one-on-one discussion or a gathering meeting or homeroom, concentrating on what others are stating enables you to introduce yourself all the more adequately. When you listen effectively, you likewise find out additional.

Check out the room during a talk, introduction, or break room. The indications of individuals not listening are all over the place. A few people put on a clear gaze that must be portrayed as their "screen-saver face" (in the expressions of one of my associates). You recognize what that screen-saver face resembles: it is that clear gaze where the eyes are dull and looking vacantly into no place and the face has definitely no demeanor on it by any stretch of the imagination. You'll additionally notice individuals in a gathering or group of spectators who do not take a gander at the speaker by any stretch of the imagination. Actually, they look wherever else.

They mess with their pencil or longingly look at their mobile phone or even attempt to sneak a look at its screen. If there is a window in the room they gaze at the sky, regardless of whether the view is only that of the neighboring place of business. An incredible speaker may charm even the most headstrong group of spectators part. The normal speaker, partner, companion, or relative may experience serious difficulties getting the look of the collected audience members who do not have a clue how to rehearse essential listening aptitudes.

If we are the speakers, we need others to tune in. So for what reason cannot a considerable lot of us play out the support backward? It is conceivable that internet based life are making numerous individuals lose their centering capacity. Generally, the normal audience requires a shift in incitement after around 20 minutes. Be that as it may, with quick fire messages coming wherever from Facebook to Twitter to push notifications from web based games, numerous individuals require a shift in incitement after maybe as short as 15 seconds. Except if you have that magnetic touch, you will experience considerable difficulties battling the consideration shortfalls of your crowd.

The issue with poor audience members is not just that they are seen as impolite yet that they pass up significant information. Investigations of the destructive impact of performing multiple tasks on understudy learning demonstrate that understudies who messaged on their cellphones, messaged, refreshed their Facebook status, and sent texts had less fortunate evaluations than the individuals who tuned in to addresses without diversion. As indicated by the "psychological bottleneck hypothesis," proposed by clinician Alan Welford in 1967, you can just process such a great amount of data on the double before your learning begins to endure.

Coming back to the inconsiderateness point of poor tuning in, individuals who do not listen likewise appear to have less fortunate social abilities when all is said in done. In an examination led in Louisiana found that understudies low in the quality they identified as "dynamic empathic tuning in" had lower scores on a social abilities stock. Being a poor audience is related with more unfortunate social and enthusiastic affectability. This was a correlational report, obviously, so we cannot decide causality. There may likewise be a third (or more) factor influencing both tuning in and social abilities. These qualifications aside, the outcomes are captivating.

Another qualification is the way this was an undergrad test, and as a matter of fact not agent of the populace. In any case, one could contend that it is especially inconvenient for individuals to pick up listening aptitudes when they are in the rising adulthood period of advancement. The social aptitudes you learn in your late youngsters and mid 20s remain with you all through life and can impact the nature of your life. If you do not build up your social aptitudes in your initial grown-up years, you'll have a harder time getting a new line of work, a sentimental partner, and an encouraging group of people you'll require as you progress through adulthood. You may even be an increasingly successful sales rep, if that is the profession you choose to seek after.

Validation

When we consider what we can do to sustain our relationship, we regularly consider physical assets. Get her precious stone hoops. Take her out to a rich supper. Shock him by wearing provocative unmentionables. Purchase blooms and chocolate. Take a sentimental excursion together. While these things surely will not hurt your relationship (by any stretch of the imagination!), they aren't really the most grounded approaches to associate with your adored one.

The more profound part has more to do with how you collaborate together as opposed to what you do together. It is called validation. Reliable, keen validation of your partner's musings and sentiments is the best thing you can accomplish for your relationship.

Recall when you felt truly comprehended. Maybe it was a minding instructor in evaluation school who appeared to know precisely the best thing to state when you were disturbed. Perhaps it is your companion who dropped everything when you called with energizing news and was anxious to share your delight. Recollect the last time you truly felt heard, comprehended, and tuned in to. It is an amazing inclination, would it say it is not?

Validation in your relationship is a similar thought. It implies that when your partner enlightens you concerning their day, or offers their sentiments, you remain with them at the time, respecting their experience. You join their reality and see things from their perspective. It is a method for demonstrating you comprehend and acknowledge their contemplations and emotions similarly as they may be. Research has demonstrated that having these kinds of collaborations with your partner helps your partner feel less annoyed and less powerless, though negating practices do the inverse; they make your partner feel scrutinized, rejected, or disdain from you.

Connections that are the best are those where the two partners share their internal world with each other - their genuine considerations, sentiments and wants - and where their partner, thus, can truly hear them. When you share an approving style of communicating together, you assemble trust and closeness. These are the bonds that make connections last.

While the idea of validation may appear to be basic, it can now and then be somewhat dubious to execute. Envision your partner gets back home and reveals to you they are irate in light of the fact that they discovered they have to work over the occasion end of the week. What is your first response? A large number of us would feel defensive of our life partner, or steamed at the circumstance, and have the common desire to attempt to help or fix the circumstance. You may offer exhortation on the most proficient method to tackle the issue. While it naturally feels supportive to give proposals, this can feel refuting to your partner. Your partner may not be searching for assistance with an answer - they most likely have effectively attempted to discover approaches to take care of the issue, and may feel considerably increasingly disappointed in hearing exhortation, regardless of how great your expectation.

So how would you viably tune in to and approve your partner? There are a couple of key parts to help direct your discussions.

1. Pose inquiries. If your partner introduces an issue or difficult circumstance to you, attempt to discover progressively about how they are feeling and what they need by asking open-finished inquiries. "What do you wish would occur?" "What was your response to that?" "How are you feeling about things currently?" Gently posing inquiries to clarify their experience can be

exceptionally gratifying for them. It demonstrates you give it a second thought and need to truly tune in.

2. Recognizing and tolerating is the following stage in validation. This implies you recognize what they've said or what they are feeling. You may state, "I can see you are vexed about this," or "You appear to be disheartened" because of their report about working throughout the end of the week. Instead of attempting to brighten your partner up, you permit them space to be disturbed.

3. Show you get it. Utilize approving explanations, for example, "I would feel that way, as well," or "It sounds good to me that you would feel that way given the conditions" to tell them you see why they feel the manner in which they do. You can likewise indicate validation with non-verbal, for example, giving them an embrace if they feel desolate, making them some tea if they feel jumpy, or giving them space if they need time to think.

4. Careful listening is the main part of validation. This implies you truly focus on what your partner is stating. As difficult as it may be, suspend your very own decisions and responses to the circumstance or theme. Incidentally let go of the need to prompt, change, help or fix the circumstance. Your own musings are set aside for later; your center, rather, is on your partner's present involvement. Show you are tuning in by halting what you are doing (shutting the PC, killing the TV), going to confront them, gesturing your head, and looking as they talk.

5. Approving doesn't approach concurring. A significant qualification is that you can acknowledge your partner's sentiments, however it doesn't mean you have to concur with them. For example, state that you head out to see a motion picture together. Subsequently, you examine your musings about the film. Your partner thought that it was engaging and interesting, while

you thought that it was exhausting and unsurprising. You may approve their perspective by saying, "It seems like you truly appreciated the film. It wasn't my top choice, yet I can tell that you had a ton of fun watching it." In this model, you are recognizing your partner's delight in something, without having a similar supposition.

At last, it is about the manner in which you collaborate together, significantly more so than what you do together. Also, it can have a significant effect in your relationship.

Chapter 4 – Break the Patterns

Denial

A great many people have an assortment of self-sabotaging practices that keep them from manifesting the life that they need. The initial phase in beating self-sabotaging practices is to initially remember them. One of the most dominant self-sabotaging practices is refusal.

Refusal is a barrier system that releases uneasiness and enthusiastic distress. By denying there is an issue we do not need to feel terrible about the way that there is an issue. Sadly this doesn't tackle anything or improve our lives. It just hides our issues where no one will think to look. They're still there. As yet worrying us and as yet holding us up.

Sometimes we deny our own well being when we fail to acknowledge and tend to a problem currently affecting us. Tragically when it turns into the obvious issue at hand, something we never again can deny, it turns into an issue considerably more difficult to determine than had we recognized it and confronted it when it previously showed up.

One type of denial is denying that our practices are really self-sabotaging. For instance, when we are late for an arrangement we may disclose to ourselves that it will not make any difference, that the reason we give will be acknowledged and that there will not be any negative results. However, this typically is not valid. When we are late for arrangements or do not get back to individuals in time, it will end up ruining your reputation over time and you will be unable to recover he same respect they once had for you.

Living in the Past

Living before and not recognizing what would be inevitable is a type of forswearing. Regardless of whether you figure pot ought to be authorized and whether you figure gay marriage ought to be sanctioned, what would be inevitable is that these things will one day all around happen and to deny this and battle this is extremely a gigantic exercise in futility, vitality and assets that could best be spent somewhere else.

Another type of refusal is denying that pardoning, acknowledgment and love have the ability to move mountains. The vast majority accept that outrage and hostility are the best approach to take care of issues. In the short run this may appear to be the situation however over the long haul they are most certainly not. Love is a phenomenal power that can change. At the point when two individuals are battling with one another, if one individual can transcend the war zone and express obvious genuine acknowledgment, pardoning and love, it generally can release all the cynicism and reestablish harmony in the relationship.

A great many people imagine that pardoning is an indication of weakness. They do not accept that the quiet will acquire everything of importance. This is refusal. Pardoning is an impression of incredible quality and individual power. Survival of the fittest will one day demonstrate to be survival not of the physically fittest yet of the profoundly fittest: the individuals who decide not to battle and rather demand finding quiet goals.

We harm ourselves with disavowal and in different ways also in light of the fact that at an oblivious level we are loaded up with blame, disgrace and self-hatred. At an oblivious level, we accept we are undeserving and shameful of joy, wellbeing and achievement, and that our intuitive personality, accepting what we are ourselves at an oblivious level, accepting that we merit discipline and not compensate, manifests in reality that "truth" by making us do things that impede us and produce disappointment.

Accusing Others and Seeing Ourselves as Victims

Shakespeare once expressed, "The shortcoming dear Brutus lies not in our stars yet ourselves that we are subordinates." So one type of forswearing would feel that the issue lies outside of ourselves and that we are casualties of a threatening, tumultuous universe out of our control, instead of us being the prime movers of our destiny.

This is an extremely amazing type of forswearing, accusing other individuals and conditions for our difficulties. For instance when we rear end and get into an auto crash we tend to consider it a mishap when it is really the consequence of our misguided thinking and we will in general accuse the vehicle before us for halting unexpectedly.

This is regular to accuse others and not assume liability for our activities. Customarily when couples battle, one partner will accuse the other partner, expressing that "You irritated me. You made me toss the toaster against the divider. You made me shout at you. You made me hit you. If you hadn't irritated me; if you hadn't pushed my catches; if you hadn't considered me that name; if you hadn't incited me, at that point I wouldn't have acted that way." Denial for this situation is the forswearing of possession. It doesn't make a difference if we are incited. We have a decision to carry on effectively and respectably or not and if we do not, and do not let it out then we are trying to claim ignorance.

Forswearing is normal with drunkards and addicts. "If I simply have one beverage it will not generally matter. I'll have the option to deal with it - it will not grow into a difficult issue." Alcoholics and addicts reveal to themselves this in spite of having a background marked by one beverage or one medication hit growing into a major issue.

Another type of refusal with respect to liquor and medications is that individuals generally persuade themselves that other individuals do not have the foggiest idea when they are high. This is typically never the case. The vast majority can tell when other individuals are impaired.

We are willfully ignorant when we misuse other individuals and disclose to ourselves that they'll get over it, they're not going to leave us. For the most part, at some point or another, they do, and when they do there is frequently a lot of no problem, an excessive amount of developed disdain and outrage for the relationship to be fixed.

We are trying to claim ignorance when we continue putting off legitimate eating routine and exercise. The disavowal part is not that we are denying these are significant activities however that it will not one day get up to speed with us and put us in the grave rashly. We deny the long haul outcomes of our activities.

Shooting the Messenger

When somebody reveals to us something we would prefer not to hear or manage, we discover approaches to assault them and refute them with the goal that we do not need to recognize that they've made a valid statement. We may disclose to them that "You do it, as well." And so this enables us to preclude the significance from claiming us getting our very own home all together paying little heed to how other individuals carry on.

Seeing someone when we tell our partner that "I do not have any issue. I needn't bother with outrage the board. You are the one with the issue not me. You are the person who needs treatment not me," this is disavowal in spades and is a certain flame indicator of a relationship that will never mend and will in all probability one day crumble. This is another case of shooting the delivery person.

Another type of forswearing is classified "scorn before examination," which means we prejudge and dismiss a thought without first assessing it to decide whether it may have legitimacy. "That is not getting down to business." "It is an exercise in futility." These are opinionated refusals that have no premise in all actuality since we really haven't took a gander at the information.

Another type of forswearing is "doing likewise and anticipating different outcomes." Some individuals allude to this as craziness.

When we are told something that is valid that we would prefer not to hear or manage and we search out individuals who will yes us and bolster our position, this is refusal. Because we can discover a lot of individuals who disclose to us we're correct doesn't mean we're correct.

"I'm just joking" is a type of refusal. When we express something to someone that is frightful and they respond adversely, we retreat and guarantee that "I was just joking." Sometimes it is not refusal, we realize that we weren't joking and that we were making a brutal point, yet in many cases we con ourselves into accepting that we truly were just joking, we were just prodding, we implied no genuine mischief and that the individual was in effect excessively delicate. This keeps us from taking a gander at our conduct dispassionately and rectifying it.

So if self-damage and forswearing are simply the aftereffect of blame, disgrace and hating, at that point the best approach to end self-harm and refusal is to adore ourselves and pardon ourselves. The best approach to adore ourselves and pardon ourselves is to cherish others, excuse others and be of administration to other people. The more we do this, the more we send the message to our intuitive personality that we are great, adoring creatures who merit satisfaction and achievement, and the more the subliminal personality shifts its motivation. It quits murmuring pessimistic messages in our ears, it quits urging us to take part in self-sabotaging practices, and it encourages us to pull in constructive individuals and conditions in our lives that will remunerate as opposed to rebuffing.

Low Self-Esteem

Low self-esteem and cynicism can make it difficult to acknowledge obligation and useful analysis, which can upset you from circumstances and furthermore keep you from taking on new challenges; therefore, blocking you from having satisfying encounters in life. It can likewise destroy significant connections. Low self-esteem, which influences our feelings, our considerations, and conduct, just as presentations how we see and associate with ourselves as well as other people, can happen for some, reasons, including dissatisfaction from individuals you esteem, placing your self-worth in conditions that are out of your control, which when they do not go the manner in which you need makes you feel like a disappointment, and some psychological issue, for example, marginal character issue and wretchedness.

With regards to poor self-esteem, there are a few things you can do to help beat it and be the individual you were intended to be, including:

Give Back

Giving, volunteering, and helping other people that are less blessed, not just helps take the concentration off your own issues, however it additionally makes you feel great realizing you are helping other people.

Deal with Yourself

Basic things like scrubbing down, brushing your hair, wearing clean garments, eating right, and practicing consistently help you rest easy thinking about yourself. Concentrates additionally demonstrate that creation your living space agreeable, spotless and appealing likewise help improve your disposition.

Encircle Yourself with the Right People

Low self-esteem as a rule starts right off the bat in life on account of disliking specialist figures. For example, if you were always informed that you do not measure up or you were scrutinized for all that you did, it can keep you from developing into a certain grown-up with a positive self-picture.

Try not to Compare Yourself to Others

Psychotherapists caution that correlations just lead to a negative self-picture, which can prompt poor self-esteem, stress, and tension that thus can destroy your work, connections, and physical and psychological well-being.

Become acquainted with Yourself/Become Your Own Best Friend

In spite of your differences, you are profitable and have the right to like yourself. In this way, invest energy alone and set aside effort to become more acquainted with yourself, which will enable you to find where you are one of a kind, unique, and commendable, which will enable you to increase a superior valuation for yourself. You can likewise take a stab at making a rundown of your accomplishments and qualities to help yourself to remember your accomplishments, and after that audit it at whatever point you need self-esteem and need to rest easy thinking about yourself.

This is additionally an extraordinary time to pinpoint and go up against any negative perspectives that you have about yourself.

Rehash Positive Affirmations

Similarly as negative attestations, for example, you are inept, can be accepted, they can likewise be unbelieved. Accordingly, analysts propose that you rehash positive insistences that you need to accept about yourself day by day to help get you back in good shape to a period before you had low-self esteem. Indeed, inquire about demonstrates that positive insistences can even help decrease side effects of gloom and the sky is the limit from there.

Recognize Where You Need Change

We as a whole have issues; notwithstanding, if you do not perceive and recognize where you need change, it can keep you trapped in an endless cycle of poor self-esteem, which will just deteriorate the more you attempt to keep running from it. Rather, become mindful of and recognize where you need change and afterward set forth the push to improve it. You can even enroll a decent companion or relative for help.

You ought to likewise end up mindful when you are excessively reproachful of yourself, and afterward advise yourself that these are not certainties, which will help you stay away from negative feelings that can prompt negative self-talk.

At last, individuals with a positive self-gratefulness are available to progress and increasingly significant encounters, which means they do not depend on outer fortifications, for example, status or salary, for self-worth, which empowers them to encounter more joy and have a great time life. In this manner, be aware of who you permit into your life just as the conditions you permit to manage your self-worth. You ought to likewise be careful to deal with yourself, including activity and eating ideal, to help keep your both your body and your mind sound.

Compliance

This post has been extremely difficult to compose. Not on the grounds that pondering back my relationship works up an entire arrangement of feelings: outrage; sharpness; disappointment; upset and now alleviation, yet mainly in light of the fact that it is extremely difficult to articulate that time. It is difficult to verbalize, in a way that doesn't make me sound sensational and powerless, what my relationship resembled.

If there are two key exercises that I have learned they are that:

Dangerous connections can sneak up on anybody.

My ex and I were as one for a long time. In spite of the fact that there were unobtrusive pieces of information at an early stage, I was heedless to them and could never have anticipated that our relationship would turn out the manner in which it did.

Psychological mistreatment, and I do delay at calling this maltreatment, can be unpretentious and practically difficult to analyze and seldom unmistakable to those outside of the relationship.

This drove me to address myself and to accept that everything was my deficiency and in my very own head.

Here are a few highlights of my relationship:

His analysis was interminable.

Regularly it was simply little things: he didn't care for my nails to be excessively long or painted in light of the fact that "they look like paws"; I was not talkative and active enough with companions at gatherings; I ought to accomplish more exercise; we should look for his sister's recommendation on beautifying our home since "she has an extremely inventive eye". She may well have an innovative eye, yet this was our home, our home, my home and my home. He said that I was passionate and hormonal after labor and not equipped for settling on a reasonable choice. He demanded addressing my mom, inferring that she was fit for the consistent idea that I could not summon.

In open things were altogether different. Perfect suitor was on structure "Pen is an exceptionally gifted craftsman", "Pen was unemotional during work".

Truth be told understanding it now it sounds snobby and insignificant, yet when the little day by day evaluate develops and you feel like each easily overlooked detail you do could utilize improvement in your partner's eyes you are not being esteemed as an equivalent, and you are surely not being adored unequivocally.

He utilized his 'feelings' to control me.

My ex said that he would "fault, resent and dislike me for the remainder of our lives" if I didn't agree to a Catholic dedicating for our child. These words, his face and the recreation center that we were strolling in at the time will be always engraved in my brain. He at that point cried. He said that our child must be dedicated a Catholic since his dad had changed over to Catholicism on his passing bed fourteen years back.

Yet, my ex never goes to Church, he is a divorcé who hitched ten years back to get his now ex a visa to remain in the UK, we lived together and had an infant without any father present. These are not the activities of a Catholic. In any case, I could not challenge my ex on this point since I felt regretful about his Dad's passing. I could not address him during his overflowing of misery.

He put down my convictions.

My ex yelled that my absence of religion was 'a vacuum', 'a void' in me and that I could always be unable to interface or to completely comprehend being otherworldly and to accept.

Presently do not misunderstand me, it is incredible when our partners can challenge us into intriguing discourses and give us better approaches for taking a gander at the world. This is the thing that I need from a relationship. It is not incredible when they make you feel senseless, or moronic, or little, or deficient, or they reliably attempt to alter your perspective on something critical to you and which you have faith in. It deteriorates when they intentionally disregard your perspectives, over-rule you as well as go despite your good faith.

Receptiveness to new experience is incredible, however a controlling partner doesn't consider it to be a two-way road, and just needs you to figure increasingly as they do.

He made me so tired of contending that I needed to yield.

I stay away from struggle. I know this. I have to show signs of improvement at it. I got depleted rapidly from any 'talk' so would yield. Consistence was simpler... until it got to an issue where his wants were so absolutely inconsistent with my conviction framework and his dangers were obvious to such an extent that I could not consent any more. I needed to end it.

He had a terrifying temper.

He never hit me, yet he would regularly hit his clench hand against the table directly before where I was sitting. If we were in the vehicle he would quicken hard so the riggings were shouting and after that pummel his foot on the brake. He previously did this from the get-go in the relationship the morning after I had would not get in the vehicle with him since he had been drinking. That was a piece of information in those days, a sign which I overlooked. He did this in January a year ago while our infant, Cygnet, was in the back of the vehicle. By at that point, it was excessively.

I am out of the relationship now. All things considered, I am out of the relationship in a sentimental sense. We will have a co-child rearing relationship as long as we both will live.

What panics me the most presently, is that I will not have the option to pass judgment on whether the following individual I meet is a comparative sort of controlling person. I realize that our control/consistence dynamic crawled up on me. The harmful idea of our relationship snuck up on me. By what means will I see it coming?

This is the reason I do not figure I can even consider getting into another relationship yet. I do not have the confidence in my own quality of brain to have the option to identify and follow up on the signs.

I do not have a clue about that I ever will.

One of the most well-known and unsafe propensities that I see in couples and even long haul relationships is the prevalent conduct of advising your partner what they need to hear as opposed to what you need, need, think and feel. When we oblige our partner as opposed to connect on a genuine and valid level, it constructs a marriage with precarious stilts that can topple whenever.

Satisfying, accommodating people and consistence are common. So for what reason is this propensity so unavoidable?

There are numerous elements why we tell others what we think they need to hear, particularly our partner.

- Danger of being rebuked

- Dread of dismissal

- Do not have the foggiest idea how to define limits

- Shirking of awkward sentiments

- We like satisfying others, particularly those we adore

- We do not have the foggiest idea what we truly need so we come

- Maintain a strategic distance from strife or a contention

- Scared by another's responses

It is only simple—until it is most certainly not.

It may not generally be anything but difficult to react with a certifiable and fair reaction, yet nobody can make a flourishing and upbeat relationship without genuineness. Trust is based on genuineness.

There are no solid connections without every individual being consistent with themselves first. When we go along or please for a portion of the above reasons, it is improbable that we are flourishing in our relationship. Why? Since we start feeling imperceptible like we do not make a difference to the next individual despite the fact that we're the ones making that experience. It is likewise implausible that our needs or objectives get cultivated—at any rate not so quick. Nor do we get the help or delight of sharing the voyage of our development and yearnings if we're continually agreeing to our partner.

When I was first hitched, I made every effort to abstain from disquieting my better half. In addition to the fact that I sought to satisfy him (before myself), yet I additionally pushed down my wants and supplanted them with his. At that point when we had kids, my days were loaded up with fulfilling everybody. Despite the fact that my conduct gave off an impression of being chipping away at the surface, inside, I felt empty, and each trade appeared to be somewhat of a trick. Furthermore, despite the fact that individuals saw me as a friendly, kind individual, I understood that genuine thoughtfulness needed to likewise be benevolent and wanting to me.

Related perusing: Why Being a People Pleaser Damages Relationships—and What to Do About It!

There is a Difference among Kindness and Pleasing

Consideration is not thoughtful except if it is additionally kind to YOU. Individuals who look to satisfy others without considering their very own needs take a major slip up for a few reasons.

1) If we do not appear in our associations with what we think, want, and need, there is no legitimate correspondence. When we retain our fact from others, people around us are following up on incorrect, fragmented, or unhelpful data that has results regardless of whether they are indistinct at the time.

2) Even if you think you have a quite smart thought of who your partner is, I would rather not break it to you—you are not a mind reader! Perhaps the greatest grumbling I get notification from the two people in an affection relationship is that their partner attempts to reveal to them what they think or how they feel, or even attempt to talk for them. We cannot realize what is happening in someone else regardless of to what extent we've been as one. Intriguing suppositions without getting limits closeness, comprehension, and association. Thinking we KNOW what our partner thinks or feels acts like a messy channel that stains and foils important discussions. This propensity for expecting likewise flares contentions.

3) When an individual is an inactive member in a relationship, the wellbeing and essentialness of the association cannot bloom since it is unjust. A lot of falls on one individual and the relationship does not have the uniqueness that could be made by the full commitment and move of the two individuals. Also, here and there, the relationship will even sink into turning into the meaning of that word everybody severely dislikes: codependent.

4) When we fully trust our partner's pledge and accept what they guide us to be valid yet they are retaining their genuine emotions, inclinations or aversions, love's potential is repudiated and the shallowness takes from conceivable outcomes. One minute, one experience can transform us! One keen discussion can shift how we see the world and one another. Try not to pass up this beautiful association by telling your partner what you think they need to hear rather than what you truly mean and need to state.

5) Whenever an individual concurs with untruthfulness or to assuage, the two individuals in the relationship leave a circumstance or discussion with different deductions and comprehension, which once in a while has positive results. These trades will in general

make ready for misconception in future connections. It very well may be as straightforward as telling your partner that their spaghetti sauce is delectable when you truly believe it is excessively harsh or sweet.

It is every individual's obligation to step up to the plate bat for their very own needs in a relationship.

Pleasers debilitate themselves and the relationship by putting their partner at the disservice of blended messages or negligible understanding. Consistence and exploitative reactions are ruinous on the grounds that they just make a fantasy of association or understanding.

In solid and develop connections, we please others most when we are consistent with ourselves.

At exactly that point would we be able to give and get from a free and cherishing space.

Control

Seeing someone, there is normally somewhat of a battle for who has the advantage. With control issues over who will be the more prevailing figure, a little clash of the genders may begin. Ladies regularly need to demonstrate their freedom and demonstrate that they are similarly as solid as men. In the interim, men need the power and high ground as well. So here are a few different ways that you can be in charge or addition control without giving the relationship a chance to endure subsequently.

Instructions to Be in Control in a Relationship

Set Boundaries

You likely have your very own arrangement of principles that fall inside your customary range of familiarity, so it is imperative to keep a portion of those when you are seeing someone. If you do not have limits and you feel the requirement for more control, attempt and set a few. Know your points of confinement and talk them obviously to your partner. Furthermore, ensure your partner realizes that no methods no and approves your choice with steady fair articulations.

Have Self Respect

Nobody else will have regard for you if you do not have it for yourself. Seeing someone, regard is basic, so demonstrate your partner you regard yourself. Take care by the way you talk about yourself, how you handle power and how you see your character. This will all be reverberated back by your partner.

Keep up Your Independence

Continuously try to demonstrate your partner you are your very own individual. It is beneficial to have your very own side interests and companions to invest your energy with outside of the relationship. This is a decent method for how to be in charge in a relationship since it demonstrates that you are alright with yourself.

Demonstrate Your Confidence

Having certainty is alluring, and if you have faith in yourself, at that point being in charge ought to be simpler. Demonstrate your partner that you merit the best. This kind of certainty will enable you to have more power in a relationship. If you are battling with certainty, attempt to recall what is most essential to you and that you are significant and meriting. At that point, radiate this in your relationship to help increase a touch of control.

Attempt to Be Unavailable

Without messing around, ensure your partner realizes you have a life outside of the relationship. This is particularly significant in the first place with the goal that they do not think you are excessively poor. Demonstrate to them that you cherish yourself, that you can finish yourself without them, and that your relationship adds to the fantastic life you as of now have. This will help you in making sense of how to be in charge in a relationship.

Act Consistent with Your Words

There are numerous ways for how to be in charge in a relationship. If you need to be paid attention to additional by your partner and increase more control, at that point try to finish your words. Your partner will feel the difference and regard you more if you act steady with your remarks. Likewise, you need to try to finish and act when you are having a contention with your partner. If you state there will be sure repercussions, at that point ensure you stand firm. Your partner will not pay attention to you if you generally give in against your promise. It works the equivalent for keeping guarantees; make a point to be straightforward and do what you state.

Use Silence During Conflict

At the point when your partner is harming you somehow or another or being out of line, attempt to remain quiet instead of demonstrating that you lose control of your feelings so rapidly. Your partner will acknowledge they do not have as much control over you if you do not respond so rapidly to clashes. If you are considering how to be in charge in a relationship, attempt to get things done in different ways if it is not working. By taking the peaceful, quiet approach, you will find your partner napping, which may help shift the power balance.

Utilize Your Voice

Make some noise and be clear about what you need out of your partner. If they regard you, it will mean a ton to them that you are forthright and legitimate. By imparting obviously, you will demonstrate that you are in charge. This will likewise make you feel progressively enabled.

Treat Others How You Want to Be Treated

The great good old brilliant guideline of treating others how you need to be dealt with is a decent method to get regard from your partner. This will likewise enable you to increase some control that you may have lost. It demonstrates that you are responsible for your conduct and decisions and that you pay attention to it.

Try not to Settle for Less

Demonstrate your partner that you are certain and realize what you merit. If one partner can pull off anything, at that point the other's capacity is lost. It is essential to support yourself and hold your ground. Additionally, if something is not working out the manner in which you need, do not be reluctant to leave. Show you have authority over your feelings and decisions.

Try not to Waste Time with Games

A grown-up relationship is one where the control is adjusted, and if you attempt and mess around, at that point you are disturbing the power balance. You likewise would prefer not to date somebody who likes to play and is great at those games since it frequently will prompt them removing control from you. Increase control in your relationship by indicating you do not have to go into a power battle through immature games.

Talk about the Power Struggle

Before you bounce into ends or think the most exceedingly awful, attempt and examine with your partner that you need the control to be increasingly adjusted. Go through models and represent what you expect in the relationship. Offer with your partner that you need to feel that the control is not uneven.

Avoidance

Avoidance behaviors are any moves an individual makes to escape from difficult musings and emotions. These behaviors can happen from numerous points of view and may incorporate activities that an individual does or doesn't do. Individuals with frenzy issue regularly take on avoidance behaviors to evade frightful musings, sentiments of fear, and by and large tension related manifestations.

As an individual managing frenzy and uneasiness, you may as of now be comfortable with carrying on of avoidance. These behaviors can negatively affect numerous parts of your life, including your vocation, connections, and individual interests or leisure activities. You may wind up maintaining a strategic distance from openings for work, get-togethers, and even kinships trying to keep your tension under control.

Perceive When It is Happening

So as to change any maladaptive behavior, you should initially begin getting to be mindful of when it is happening. Toward the part of the arrangement, stop and think about how you occupied with avoidance behaviors consistently. Record any that stick out. You may have seen how you did this in little ways. For instance, maybe you avoided a collaborator since you felt on edge about chatting with him.

When you start to reliably follow your activities, you might be astounded to discover that you are partaking in more avoidance behaviors than you recently suspected.

You may likewise see huge manners by which you occupied with avoidance, for example, taking a different course to work to maintain a strategic distance from interstate driving since it makes you feel restless. Just by endeavoring to see these activities will you be prepared to transform them.

Impacts of Avoidance Behaviors

Beside confining your life, avoidance behaviors frequently have the contrary impact than what is wanted. While in the short run you may encounter an impermanent good feeling, over the long haul, avoidance really prompts expanded tension.

When maintaining a strategic distance from spots, individuals, and occasions, the frenzy sufferer is truly attempting to make tracks in an opposite direction from her sentiments of nervousness. Nonetheless, every time she gets away from these tension actuating considerations and emotions, she is really fortifying them. She is sending the message to herself that the world is a risky spot. At last, she may turn out to be progressively scared of an ever increasing number of improvements, considering the cycle of tension to intensify.

Why Avoidance Coping Creates Additional Stress

Individuals who live with avoidance are frequently denying themselves of numerous encounters, undertakings, and associations. Frenzy related avoidance behaviors might keep you from carrying on with your life without limit. Peruse ahead for certain tips on the most proficient method to diminish your uneasiness related avoidance behaviors.

Discovering Trust and Support

The way to defeating avoidance behaviors is to keep on gradually face what you are maintaining a strategic distance from until it never again has such a hold on you. Obviously, doing so is far actually quite difficult. That is the reason it is prescribed that you do not confront recently maintained a strategic distance from circumstances alone, but instead take part in them with a confided in companion or relative close by.

Tell your companion that the circumstance you are venturing into is normally a wellspring of uneasiness. Have a reinforcement plan prepared should things go sideways. For instance, is going to a huge get-together that you would ordinarily maintain a strategic distance from, talk heretofore about what you'll require if you feel awkward. Set up your adored one to give you space if you should need a couple of minutes alone to deal with your nervousness. Maybe you will caution her that you should leave if manifestations become unmanageable. Notwithstanding your arrangement, ensure your cherished one knows about it so she will recognize what's in store should your tension emerge.

Disclosing Your Panic Disorder to Friends and Family

Note that you never ought to depend on one individual to support your sentiments of nervousness consistently. Thusly, you may incidentally make a shift in avoidance where you become excessively subject to this individual. In the long run, you will need to step into the already avoidances alone. Your adored one may at present be supporting you from a separation, yet it is just when you push ahead alone that you can really defeat your avoidance behaviors.

Create Ways to Cope With Your Anxiety

Your avoidance behaviors rotate around not having any desire to encounter uneasiness or different manifestations of frenzy issue. The best method to move beyond this dread is to learn procedures that will enable you to control your manifestations. Adapting abilities can enable you to hold your nervousness within proper limits and may even help with dealing with your fits of anxiety. Such abilities can be learned through the assistance of a specialist or all alone by utilizing self-help books.

Some basic procedures to help in adapting to uneasiness include:

Dynamic muscle unwinding

Profound breathing activities

Subjective rebuilding

Nervousness following

Expert Help Is Available

Few out of every odd frenzy issue sufferer will encounter avoidance behaviors, notwithstanding, many will find that these issues put unnecessary limitations on their lives. If you are finding that your avoidance behaviors are unmanageable and crazy, it might be an ideal opportunity to look for expert assistance. Getting proficient assistance with your side effects is in no way, shape or form a disappointment on your part. Truth be told, numerous individuals with frenzy issue have discovered that they recuperate snappier through treatment.

Numerous individuals feel on edge in their relationship, in light of the fact that their partner keeps away from enthusiastic closeness. In spite of how baffling the avoidant partner may show up, not all things can be accused on them.

Any relationship contains a dynamic between two individuals, and issues inside the relationship must be inspected with regards to the two partners. To comprehend avoidance with regards to a relationship, we should begin with a rundown of avoidant behaviors.

Identifying Avoidant Behaviors in Your Partner

Here are a few behaviors regularly shown by the "avoidant" partner:

- Not returning writings, messages, or calls

- Overlooking plans, uncommon events, or dates

- Not saying "I adore you" or different articulations of adoration

- Avoiding discussions about further duty, for example, monogamy, commitment, or marriage

- Rejecting or taunting an partner's endeavors to be nearer, or to connect on a more profound level

This behavior can be baffling, and can make the avoidant individual's partner wonder what is "off-base" with the relationship, and whether the avoidant partner even cherishes them by any stretch of the imagination. There are regularly contentions about the relationship, where one partner faults the other for not minding "enough" or demonstrating their affection in specific ways. These battles can undermine the quality of the relationship and dissolve closeness after some time.

For this situation, the avoidant individual's partner is normally thought to be "distracted" or "on edge" in the connection writing.

This implies they can act nosy and controlling when gone up against with their partner's avoidance. The possibility that the avoidant partner doesn't love them or wouldn't like to focus on them completely triggers a frenzy reaction (called connection alarm).

What to do When You Recognize Avoidance in Your Partner

The primary activity when you perceive that your partner is avoidant is to make sense of how your very own behaviors and past issues are adding to the dynamic. It can work with a couple's advisor, yet by and large, a great many people who are intuitively attracted to avoidant partners have had encounters in their initial life where a parent or other key connection figure was relationally repressed.

When they meet an avoidant partner, these individuals intuitively observe an opportunity to at last cause a relationally stunted individual to submit, and be available and mindful. These couples become caught in a follower distancer dynamic, which implies that one partner seeks after the other for closeness, while different pushes away to build enthusiastic separation.

For some, individuals joined forces with avoidant individuals, it tends to be exceptionally valuable to inspect their very own reactions to the avoidant behavior, and make sense of if they are useful or not. For example, messaging your partner multiple times straight to disclose to them how harmed you are that they haven't reacted to you yet is not typically an accommodating behavior. This can make the avoidant individual feel focused, overpowered, and assaulted. So what would it be a good idea for you to do?

Tolerating Your Partner for Who They Are

The way in to a fruitful association with an avoidant partner is to acknowledge what their identity is, while remaining consistent with what you need. This doesn't mean what you need — which may at the time be a steady, progressing content discussion that keeps going 16 waking hours — however what you have to feel like nothing is wrong with the world and sound, which could be an partner who can say "I cherish you," or one who doesn't avoid plans.

If the avoidant partner attempts to react to your essential connection needs, do not be hesitant to part of the arrangement. In any case, if they are attempting to address your issues yet have their very own issues to work through, this may not really flag that things will not work out.

The follower distancer dynamic is normal, and it doesn't need to imply that your relationship is damned. A specialist can enable you to recognize which of the relationship issues are fundamentally because of your frailties, and which are because of your partner's example of passionate avoidance.

Fortify Your Relationship with Couples Therapy

Most relationship issues are, as you may figure, because of the unpredictable transaction between these connection styles, which can frequently be investigated gainfully with a couples instructor. Regardless of whether a cheerful relationship appears to be far away now, numerous issues can be effectively explored with the assistance of an expert.

Recovery Reminders

The facts confirm that affection is unselfish. When we have youngsters, their requirements need to precede our own. We are not going to give our infant a chance to weep for a considerable length of time from appetite in the night since we want to rest when the infant would prefer to be alert and eating. We will drive our kids around to exercises when we are drained or would prefer to accomplish something different. Acting capably as a parent is a piece of loving our kids.

In any case, when we generally put the other first in our grown-up connections, to the detriment of our own wellbeing or prosperity, we might be codependent.

About Codependency

Codependency is a scholarly behavior. We watch the activities of our folks when we are kids. If our mom or father had an issue with limits, was consistently the saint, would never say 'no' to individuals, and had unfortunate approaches to impart, we doubtlessly took in these behaviors and brought them into our private connections.

Youngsters who grow up with relationally stunted guardians likewise are in danger for being codependent. They regularly wind up seeing someone where their partner is relationally stunted, yet they remain in the expectations that they can change the individual. Regardless of what occurs, they will not quit trusting that one day things will be great.

The subliminal expectation is that the other individual will see all the affection we give and be motivated to change. We accept that if we simply hold tight and give our affection, comprehension, and backing, we will at long last get the adoration that we wanted from our folks. This reasoning is damaging if we do not have solid limits that shield us from physical or enthusiastic mischief and sign to our partner that their harsh behavior is not satisfactory.

The most noticeably terrible part is the point at which we do not understand what is happening and keep on living in a cold association since we have never realized what a decent organization resembles. Codependent individuals do not accept that they are deserving of adoration, so they settle for less. Frequently, they end up taking mental, passionate, physical, and even sexual maltreatment from their partner.

Individuals who are codependent frequently search for things outside of themselves to feel much improved.

They structure connections that are not beneficial, hoping to 'fix' the other individual. An individual with codependent propensities may end up in a close association with an individual who has addiction issues that reason them to be relationally repressed. Their partner or they themselves might be obsessive workers or build up some other urgent behavior to maintain a strategic distance from the sentiment of vacancy in the relationship. This is simpler in the present moment than glimpsing inside and managing feelings.

The most effective method to Tell if You are Codependent

If you are seeing someone you think might be codependent, the initial step to freedom is to quit taking a gander at the other and investigate yourself.

If you genuinely state that you concur with the accompanying articulations, you might be codependent.

You will in general love individuals that you can pity and protect.

You feel in charge of the activities of others.

You accomplish more than your offer in the relationship to keep the harmony.

You fear being surrendered or alone.

You feel in charge of your partner's joy.

You need endorsement from others to pick up your own self-worth.

You experience issues acclimating to change.

You experience issues settling on choices and regularly question yourself.

You are hesitant to confide in others.

Your mind-sets are constrained by the contemplations and sentiments of people around you.

Codependency is regularly found in individuals with marginal character issue (BPD), despite the fact that this doesn't mean all individuals with codependency issues additionally meet the criteria for a conclusion of BPD.

The Relationship Between Codependency and Addiction

One of the numerous issues with a codependent relationship is that you might be accidentally empowering an partner's addiction.

In your endeavor to demonstrate your affection by "helping" your partner, you can demoralize that person from looking for the treatment important to get calm.

For instance:

You justify your better half's drinking by saying he has had an unpleasant day or requirements to unwind.

You rationalize when your better half cannot come to social capacities since she is affected by heroin.

You let your sweetheart acquire your remedy narcotics at whatever point he gripes of any minor distress, despite the fact that you are stressed over his developing reliance on the prescription.

You discreetly take on additional obligations around the house or in child rearing your kids on the grounds that your partner is constantly impaired.

You wind up much of the time saying 'sorry' to other people or doing favors to fix connections harmed by your partner's medication or liquor misuse.

You hazard your own monetary future by advancing cash to your partner to cover obligations brought about from substance misuse.

Addiction weakens judgment and basic reasoning aptitudes. This makes it extremely difficult for somebody with a substance use issue to see that the person in question needs assistance. When you make a special effort to keep your partner from encountering the outcomes of substance misuse, you make it more outlandish that the individual will recognize that an issue exists.

Cherishing somebody with a substance use issue can likewise cause your codependent propensities to winding crazy. At the point when your partner is acting whimsically because of medication or liquor misuse, it is anything but difficult to fall back on utilizing codependent behavior in your battle to keep up a feeling of authority over turbulent environment. This makes an endless loop that traps both of you in a dysfunctional and unfortunate relationship.

Recuperating from Codependency

Fortunately, codependency is a scholarly behavior, which means it very well may be unlearned. If you cherish your partner and need to keep the relationship, you have to mend yourself as a matter of first importance.

Some sound strides to recuperating your relationship from codependency include:

Start being straightforward with yourself and your partner. Doing things that we would prefer not to do not just burns through our time and vitality, yet it additionally expedites feelings of hatred. Making statements that we do not mean just harms us, since we at that point are carrying on a falsehood. Be straightforward in your correspondence and in communicating your needs and wants.

Stop negative reasoning. Catch yourself when you start to think adversely. If you start to imagine that you have the right to be dealt with seriously, get yourself and change your musings. Be sure and have higher desires.

Try not to think about things literally. It takes a ton of work for a codependent individual not to think about things literally, particularly when in a private relationship. Tolerating the different as they are without attempting to fix or change them is the initial step.

Take breaks. There is nothing amiss with taking a break from your partner. It is beneficial to have companionships outside of your association. Going out with companions takes us back to our inside, helping us to remember who we truly are.

Think about guiding. Get into guiding with your partner. An instructor fills in as an impartial outsider. They can call attention to codependent inclinations and activities among you that you may not know about. Input can give a beginning stage and bearing. Change cannot occur if we do not change.

Depend on companion support. Mutually dependent people Anonymous is a 12-advance gathering like Alcoholics Anonymous that encourages individuals who need to break free of their codependent behavior designs.

Set up limits. The individuals who battle with codependency frequently experience difficulty with limits. We do not have the foggiest idea where our needs start or where the opposite's end. We regularly flourish off blame and feel terrible when we do not put the other first.

Self-Care Is Not Selfish

As you are attempting to break the cycle of codependency, it might appear as though you are being urged to act in way that is selfish and out of line to your partner. This could not possibly be more off-base.

In a sound relationship, the two individuals have full grown characters outside of their time together. They each carry exceptional ascribes to the table—making an association that enables them two to develop and flourish.

Watching a friend or family member battle with medication or liquor addiction is tragic, yet you will not be in any situation to help your partner's addiction treatment except if you set aside a few minutes to address your own emotional wellness needs.

Conclusion

Thank you for making it through to the end of *Codependency Recovery Guide*, let's hope it was informative and able to provide you with all of the tools you need to achieve your goals whatever they may be.

The next step is to like us on social media and spread the word on the relevance of the book to others in difficult relationships.

Narcissistic Abuse Healing Guide

Follow the Ultimate Narcissists Recovery Guide, Heal and Move on from an Emotional Abusive Relationship! Recover from Narcissism or Narcissist Personality Disorder!

By Victoria Hoffman

Introduction

Congratulations on purchasing *Narcissistic Abuse Healing Guide: Follow the Ultimate Narcissists Recovery Guide, Heal and Move on From an Emotional Abusive Relationship! Recover From Narcissism or Narcissist Personality Disorder!* Today, we get to interact with people with different personalities in many areas of life including work, school, and relationships. Unfortunately, some of us have interacted with generally unhappy and disappointed people who lack self-esteem and lack empathy for others—the so-called narcissists. Victims of narcissism may end up suffering from anxiety, stress, and depression, which contribute to other health problems. By downloading this book, you have taken the first step towards learning how to get away and recover from narcissistic abuse. The information that you find in the following chapters is very important as it will guide you to take control of your life immediately and develop a healthier mind and personality.

To that end, this book provides an in-depth overview of narcissistic personality disorder, providing a clear understanding of the character traits of narcissists, success stories of narcissistic abuse, and the healing process. It also covers the narcissistic victim mode, in which we cover the circumstances surrounding a narcissistic victim, including what makes it challenging to heal from the abuse and the cornerstones of healing. The book also offers a comprehensive account of the pseudo personality and how to get rid of it Further, we propose the strategies necessary for dealing with pseudo personality, including the possible challenges and how to acknowledge that you have pseudo personality.

Many books on this subject are plenty in the market, thanks once again for considering this one! Please enjoy reading!

Chapter 1: Success Stories

In order to give love, we must all love ourselves first. This statement appears to be true that most of us fil to thoroughly examine it. In day-to-day affairs, be it business, be it love, or in the family setup, we act on this premise, yet it is shaky.

While some people believe that they do not love themselves at all (ego-dystonic group), others feel they have self-love because they are contended by who they are (ego-syntonic). Yet other people restrict their definition of love in regard to their traits, behavioral patterns, and personal history. But there appears a group of people with a unique mental constitution – the narcissists.

Introduction to Narcissistic Characters

Narcissists are believed to be in love with themselves. However, this is not the case. A narcissist is always in love with his REFLECTION rather than being in love with HIMSELF. Being in love with oneself is functional, healthy, and adaptive, but having a love for one's self-reflection is associated with two setbacks: the person always depends on the availability of the reflection in order to develop self-love and the lack of "objective and realistic yardstick" of whether the reflection exists in reality.

A common misconception is that narcissists always love themselves. But in reality, their love is always directed to others people's approval of them. A person whose love is based on impression is not capable of genuinely loving other people, including his own self.

A narcissist has an in-bred desire to feel loved and to love others, which means that if he is unable to love himself and others, he must be in love with his reflection amidst the possible contrast with his self-image. Unlike an ordinary person, a narcissist would invest a lot of energy and other resources to maintain the projected image, sometimes becoming vulnerable to external threats.

But a major trait that projects the image of a narcissist is lovability. A narcissist will always associate love with other emotions like respect, attention, awe, and admiration. Thus, for a narcissist, a projected image is usually loveable and can be loved, thus, equating it to self-love. This character drains narcissists of their mental energy, thereby lacking any left to dedicate to other people.

Success Stories of Narcissistic Abuse

I developed an interest in understanding narcissism in the year 2014 when I got a chance to visit a 3-day Narcissistic Abuse Recovery Program that was held in Brooklyn. During the event, I met several survivors of narcissistic abuse as well as those that are still trapped with narcissists. But the most intriguing story was that involving three subjects, Lilie who had separated from her narcissistic husband, Joe, and Kelly who escaped from his narcissistic family members. In this section, I am going to share their experience with narcissists, and how they recovered from the abuse.

Case Study #1: Lilie's Experience with a Narcissistic Husband

When Lilie stood before the congregation, she began to sob even before uttering a word. She seems to have put the matters behind her, but still, the wound seemed fresh. She had just walked out of her 12 years marriage and had taken her two kids to live with her mother. She narrated how she had been blinded for more than 10 years not to recognize that she was leaving with a narcissist. When she began talking, I felt a personal connection with her pain, vividly narrating how she met her husband back in the college days,

"I remember vividly how we met back in college, at the beginning of the summer. I had just joined campus and the person who was ready to give me orientation was Josh who was already a second year. That day he showed me everywhere, including the classes, the laboratories, the botanical areas, and eventually to his room where he jovially welcomed me. By the end of the day, I knew I had met a friend, and as history would have it, we soon began dating."

Lilie explained how they were always together, and Josh would take her everywhere as long as he was free. After 3 years of dating, Josh took her to meet his parents in the summer holidays, whom she saw were very nice people. However, during her stay there, she recalled observing her boyfriend being to controlling with the parents, something she had never felt (or too ignorant to notice). He would dictate what is to be cooked, how he would be treated and the help he would render to his family. When she asked about the negative attitude, he always told her, "you don't know how mean these people are, just shut up."

After they graduated, they decided to get married. Although the wedding was fabulous, Lilie recalled that Josh changed immediately they got married. He would no longer let her go out to meet her friends, telling her that she needed more time to concentrate on her newly built home. He would accompany her to the groceries and any other places she wanted to go to during the weekends, and on weekdays, he would frequently pop up to check on her without notice.

"At first, I thought that Josh just wanted to spend time with me, but I came to realize later that he was just a narcissist. When he found me talking to my male colleagues, he would intentionally engage me in a heated argument about not being dedicated to our marriage and flirting with men. He would even call me names like whore or sl**t then later apologize."

Lilie began to blame herself, feeling that she never loved Joe enough. She, therefore, resorted to not having any conversation or social engagement with her male colleagues except with her bosses. She would later abandon all her female friends and her sisters since she had believed that they were just a waste of time and that they did not add any value to the marriage. But things got even worse when she had her first born, "

"When I had my first baby, I had gained a lot of weight. Joe considered that a weakness point, and would mock me with it. He was never there for any of us, and I was left struggling alone. He was distant emotionally and sexually, and one time he told me that he lost interest in me because I was fat."

Lilie further narrated how she plunged into depression and recalled falling sick often because of stress. Joe would tell her that she preferred other women because she was no longer good enough, but she endured all the traumatizing abuses, just to keep her marriage going. She would soon get her second baby after 3 years, and the state of her marriage grew even worse.

"After our second baby, Joe wanted me to leave my career so that I can baby sit. He believed he had enough money to take care of us, so I didn't have a reason to work. But I still did not lose myself to that extend. I love my art job, and I wouldn't have sacrificed it at all. When I refused, my husband became violent; he associated my going to work to have an opportunity to meet men. I would cry throughout the night as he could abuse me before the kids. But my kids' nanny opened my eyes."

According to Lilie, she learned that her nanny had experienced such a marriage life before she decided to get divorced. Unfortunately for her (nanny), she never had a good career to move on earlier. She was abused for a long time, but when the beatings were too much, she decided to go and look for casual jobs. When Lilie heard her story, it became an eye opener to her. She noticed that truly she was living with a narcissist who had psychological issues.

She, therefore, decided to record her husband during an argument one evening. She then took the abusive recording to the court, where she filed a divorce and children's lawsuit. Eventually, she got her freedom and swore not to have such an ugly experience again.

Case Study #2: Kelly Detaches Herself from Her Narcissistic Family

"The moment I knew I had to part ways with my narc-family is when my father died," Kelly narrated her experience sorrowfully that many people in the group shed tears. She recalls how she had been so close to the father. Being a first-born child in the family, her parents held high expectations from her and wanted her to get a better education so that she could later take care of her three other siblings.

But their dream was halt when her father was diagnosed with cancer in 2014. He had been the breadwinner of his family since he was a dedicated banker and a part-time businessman. When he got sick, Kelly's mother took over the business, which she ran with her other sisters who were 23 and 25 respectively. Because of financial strains, ranging from hospital bills, house bills, to the education costs of her younger siblings, Kelly was forced to drop out of her postgraduate nursing course and went to look for an internship at a local hospital. She made efforts to contribute to the family budget as much as she can, but her mother could not appreciate any of her efforts.

"I worked both day and night because I wanted my father to get the best medication. Since his former employer did not cover him for chronic diseases, he had to resign and use whatever we generated for his hospital bills. But my mom was never there for him at all. I felt that the business was doing well and that she could support my father's treatment with no strain."

Kelly describes how her mother stopped taking care of the father, telling her constantly that she and her children needed the money more because they have more days to live. The most painful moment that Kelly remembers is how her mother constantly abused the dad for choosing a poor lifestyle,

"She blamed my dad's poor habit and excess alcohol intake to be the cause of his cancer. She even told him that he was better off dead than continue draining the less money available."

Although Kelly ensured he took care of her father, she became depressed because of the mistreatment she saw from the other members of the family. Her other siblings never bothered to offer emotional support to the dad, and would never accompany him to the hospital. They always blamed my dad for being sick and blamed me for neglecting them by focusing all my attention on my dad.

Due to the torture that his father received, he ended his life by overdosing on the prescribed cancer drugs,

"I remember that night vividly. I had taken my dad home before I went back to work in the afternoon. And when I returned home, I found the house so quiet. When I went to his room, he was lying there helplessly, with bottles of drugs scattered on the floor. But he had not pulse left."

Kelly believes that her family members were not only sadists but also narcissists because of their self-centeredness. When the dad was alive, he took care of their mom and all of the siblings. However, when he got sick, everyone turned against him and blamed him for his chronic diseases instead of offering support.

Once her dad was buried, she decided to separate herself from the family to start life in a different city. She wished things were different, but she has not been able to forgive any of them.

Chapter 2: Victim Mode

Living a life of manipulation, violation, and being lied to can have severe consequences to you as the victim. Healing from the damage the narcissist has left in you can be difficult, primarily if you blame yourself. You may ask how you could have possibly let that kind of person in your life. Someone who caused you so much pain. However, you can break the chains of manipulation and be free from them (if you still are) and heal from the damage they have caused you.

What Makes It Hard to Heal from A Narcissistic Abuse

The disparity of truth: Why is it hard to recover from the damage the narcissist has caused? Why is it so hard to get over it? It is humans' natural need to have a connection with others. To be cared for and also to give love. When others hurt you, the pain won't matter because you have that one who truly cares about you. But what happens when pain is from the one you care about? Usually, you might walk away from the pain and the person, no matter how much you care for them. But with a narcissist, things are different.

A narcissist will initially shower you with passionate love and attention; this is called love bombing. He studied you and all your trigger points. What you liked most and what you felt insecure about. He will then use that to his advantage; flatter and reassure you. It will feel good at first until it doesn't. Narcissist uses love bombing as a tool to build themselves to you as the perfect lover or friend. They intend to win you over to control you.

The thing with a narcissist relationship is that it will be difficult for you to comprehend what is happening to you. You will get addicted to his "love," and you will find yourself always seeking his attention-craving for his approval. Once you are under his control, you will notice the hurting comments here and there. You will brush it off, thinking it's a mistake. With time, you will see that the behavior seems off, and so you will blame yourself.

The Clarity in Retrospect

You can spot the signs; how he treats, how he manipulates you. You know that you deserve better. But when it comes to letting go, you think you will not survive without them. Your friends and family will even wonder why you are with such a person. However, you might find it difficult to answer because you have no valid answer.

According to psychologists, most victims of narcissists don't even know that they are in an abusive relationship. This explains why most of them stick around. People associate abuse to physical. You should understand that manipulation, gaslighting, and all forms of psychological and emotional abuse are part of violence.

According to Dr. Craig Malkin, the author of Rethinking Narcissism, the narcissist will find a way back into your life even though you might not want them. A narcissist is in a battle with themselves about whether to push you away or have you in their lives. For this reason, when you break off the relationship, they will find a way back to break it off. They don't leave without a fight.

You keep letting them back in because your mind and your heart are not on the same page. Your heart says you care about this person while your mind says they are toxic, and you should let them go. This lack of agreement may go on for months or even years without being resolved.

Learned powerlessness

Picture this situation. You are in the middle of the ocean a thousand miles away from civilization when a tragedy happens. Your boat experiences engine problems that you can't fix. You didn't carry a phone or something that could call for help. So what do you do? Nothing. Maybe sit and wait for a miracle.

Being in a narcissistic relationship is similar to being in a damaged boat in the middle of the ocean. You feel powerless because you are not in control.

Powerlessness doesn't occur abruptly in a toxic relationship. He will subject you to abusive situations. Regular insults, manipulations, and gaslighting will eventually make you feel you have no control over what is happening in your life. Over time, you will feel immobilized. You will feel unable to take care of your own needs, even those that seem simple. A narcissist will abuse you until the powerlessness becomes internalized.

Healing will be difficult when you feel powerless. You will feel you don't deserve to be happy or free from abuse.

Learned powerlessness will also make you helpless. You will be unable to speak up or seek help from those who can offer assistance. You will also be unable to trust people because of the pain and damage you experienced.

In most cases, a victim of an abusive relationship will end up in another toxic relationship if he/she does not heal. You will be attracted to people who have similar traits to your ex because you feel you don't deserve better.

The Lonely Road

A victim of a narcissistic relationship will find it hard to heal because of the lonely journey. Loneliness will start pretty early in the relationship. Your lover will isolate you from your friends and family and make you believe you are alone.

Love and attention might have driven you into the arms of an abusive partner, but lack of control might be the glue that kept you there.

A narcissistic partner who made you believe that you couldn't possibly survive without them will insert total control over your life that you feel helpless without them. His efforts would go into making you believe that life out there is difficult. Of course, this is not true unless you don't get a supportive system.

If your efforts to reach out for help go unanswered, you will get accustomed to living on your own. You will slowly realize that things will always be hard for you. That no matter what you do, you are on your own.

When your family tries to help but cannot understand your situation, ill only frustrate you leading to you pulling away. You will find yourself tolerating the pain for far too long. Victims of narcissists end up on a lonely journey of pain and shame over what they have experienced.

Fear of the Unknown

Even though the most logical thing to do would walk away from a toxic relationship, fear of the unknown will hold you back. Irrespective of how unhappy you are, your distrust of the world will make your stay in the relationship.

Fear of the unknown will keep you from healing from the harm caused by your narcissist lover. Just like loneliness, your partner will make you believe life without them is difficult. You will be conditioned to think there is nothing better for you out there.

Fear of the unknown will also make you not envision a better future for yourself. When other people envision serenity and peaceful existence for themselves, in your case, the thoughts will be so foreign. Through your partner's behavior, you will be convinced that there is nothing better for you. That the future is blank and every step you take towards it is doomed.

Trapped in fear, you will dismiss any hope of support systems available out there. You won't even consider whether other people are experiencing the same thing. When walking around, you may see happy people on the streets, but the thought that you could also be happy won't cross your mind.

A victim of a narcissistic relationship will get accustomed to the abuse until he/she believes that it is how the world is. You will tell yourself it's better to stay in a place where you are familiar, unlike the unknown. If you had a previous toxic relationship, you would resign on the thought of leaving. According to you, the world is the same.

Fear of the unknown will prevent you from forming healthy relationships and end up living in isolation.

Laying Down the Facts

You may wonder why a person would choose to stay in a place that is not conducive to them. Or why someone would want to hold to pain. The thing is when you are exposed to abuse over a long time, leaving becomes difficult.

Victims may hold on to pain or stay in a toxic relationship because of a variety of reasons — fear of leaving, for the sake of children and the idea that the partner will change. But the truth is, holding onto pain for whatever reason is not doing yourself justice.

The narcissist in your life planned everything from the word go. After he studied and new all your weak points, he hatched a plan to win you over. You ended up hooked to his "love." He needed you to be what he is. You were his target audience.

A narcissist needs an audience. So, they will cultivate relationships quickly with anyone who pays to listen. As their façade starts to slip up, and their reality starts to set in, they will try to hide their shortcomings. They fear that people will see rough their flaws to the person they are.

The narcissist has an inflated sense of self. Everything they do revolves around them. They will do everything at the expense of others. According to Jacklyn Krol, a psychotherapist and a licensed clinical social worker, narcissists talk about their accomplishments and successes with grandiose. They will also exaggerate what they have achieved to impress their audiences.

As a victim, when you finally choose to see through his façade, you will realize how shallow they are. You will notice how all the conversations you had were centered on them and their lives.

He noted how empathetic you were and choose you as his target. Most people with narcissist personality disorder have low self-esteem, according to Shirin Peykar, a Licensed Marriage and Family therapist.

Don't Expect Them to Change

The truth is people don't break easily; they only change when they want to. He is never going to be the person you wish them to be. A lot of times, you may find yourself reminiscing of the past moments, where he was sweet and loving. However, you should remember that it was all a game. A plan to win you over.

A narcissist only thinks of himself. Whatever he does is centered on his needs. You may hold onto hope, thinking he will change. You may wonder why he changed for the worst and not for the better. But something you should remember is that even though change is possible, someone has to want it.

Understand that you deserve happiness, and you expecting them to change won't help you in any way.

Most of the time, the narcissist will promise to change. This will give you hope for a while until it doesn't. Without any effort to change or seek help, his promises to change will be a way to seek control over you.

If he chooses to change, he will have to go through this process:
- He should understand that his actions are causing harm to you
- He should also despise the behavior so much to want to let it go
- When making a negative choice unknowingly, he should immediately recant it and make a better one.

- He should also know that he has a choice in every situation, including how he chooses to treat those around him.

You were never the problem: In a narcissistic relationship, victims will blame themselves for their partner's behavior, according to Jacklyn. You will say to yourself, "he was good when we meet and during our first dates. So, I must have done something that made him change." But this is not right.

People with a narcissist personality disorder don't care about other people's feelings in any way. So quit blaming yourself for his behavior. You were never a problem.

Narcissists exhibit a grandiose image of themselves. They think they only matter and that they should only be associated with people of a higher class than them. Narcissists seek admiration from those around them, which is why he will exaggerate his achievements and accomplishments.

Narcissistic personality disorder might be inborn or acquired. Usually, this happens during childhood. If his parents or guardians were critically harsh towards him, that could be the cause. According to Heinz Kohut, a psychoanalyst in a study on his clients, he observed the following: Narcissists went through a life of alienation, helplessness, and emptiness. They lacked the structures to form stable and meaningful relationships and a positive self-perception.

When they have a negative image of themselves, shame sets in, and they take it out on others. The degrade others to feel good about themselves. They project their insecurities through the manipulation of others, especially those close to them. For the victims that not aware of this, they end up blaming themselves.

You shouldn't feel sorry for him/her: For an empathetic person, it is reasonable to feel sorry for people around you, including your narcissist lover/friend. However, you should remember that people with a narcissist personality disorder suffered an emotional injury from an early age. For this reason, they are incapable of feeling sorry for anyone but themselves. You may not believe that the person who showed you kindness and sympathy would turn out to be a narcissist.

A lot of times, victims of a narcissist will try to apologize for their wrongdoings. Usually, this happens when they notice your attempts to leave them. They will plead with you to leave them.

A narcissist will use manipulation to have their way with the target audience and avoid any accountability. Once you understand how a narcissist mind works, you will not feel sorry for his actions.

The narcissist knows what they are doing: The reality is every person has a bit of narcissism in them. But for the narcissist, they score higher than the rest of us. Their move is carefully planned and executed.

Every person makes a mistake, and what differentiates a narcissist from the rest is the unwillingness to take charge of their choices. Typically, when a person makes a mistake, they take responsibility and humbly apologize for it. However, the narcissist doesn't even say sorry when they wrong you. He will choose to offer a fake apology to get on the right side with you.

But the real question is, does he change after the apology? The truth is, when a narcissist apologizes, he does so for himself and not because he cares about your feelings.

According to the author of healing from hidden abuse, Shannon Thomas, emotional and psychological abusers, know what they are doing. They know the right buttons to press. They know when to turn off their manipulative tendencies. They know what to do to get a response from their victims. This shows that they are intelligent beings — people who know what they are doing.

The Cornerstone of Healing

Understand that it is possible to heal. Most victims of a narcissist relationship find it hard to recover because of the damage to their self-esteem. As mentioned earlier, healing is possible. Here is what you should do first:

Ask Why

Asking yourself why this happened to you will open up a lot of doorways into things you have never known. For instance, why you were his target. When you ask these questions, you will get a lot of insights that will help prevent a similar situation in the future. Similarly, it will create a chance for you to choose to heal.

When you understand why you were the target, you will find ways to strengthen your weaknesses. This means, in the future, you can see through a person's fakeness.

Be Specific

When you look into why you were the victim; it is wise to be accurate on what exactly made you the target. Is it you empathetic. Were you desperate for love and attention? Narcissists study their victims first before making a move. So, it is best to know what exactly triggered him to you.

Be Kind to Yourself

It's important not to blame yourself because of the actions of the abusers. When you understand that some things are beyond your control, you will find it easier to heal and let go.

Narcissist actions are solely based on his desires, even though he chooses you has his victim, understand it has nothing to do with you.

Be Smart

When healing happens, you will be more careful about the kind of people you let close to you. You will no longer entertain love bombing from a love interest. You can choose to walk away when the relationship shows signs of any manipulation. It means you can tell a person to back off when everything is about them.

Being smart in the decisions you make will help you in a great way. Besides healing, you will be able to understand a lot about different human personalities. It is essential to deal with past hurts and forgive yourself so that you can move forward.

Stay on Top

No man is an island. Go out and meet new people. You can seek the help of support groups, which will help you in the recovery journey. Just like any other problem, yours has a solution, and healing is part of it.

You can also choose to be a role model to others going through a similar situation. This usually happens when you trust that you have dealt with all the hurtful things.

You will also notice that when helping others, you will be able to heal all the wounds. This is because, in a support group, people will look up to you and give you respect, which you didn't get in the relationship with the narcissist. You will see that it is possible to be loved and respected.

As shown in this chapter, there are a lot of things that can make it hard for victims to deal with the narcissist in their lives. However, it is also possible for them to heal from the abuse.

Chapter 3: Getting Rid of The Pseudo Personality

As earlier discussed, the term pseudo personality refers to falsehood or pretense. Therefore, the psychology of pseudo personality is highly appended to the practice of falsehood. It is also best thought of as one that dominates a pre-cult personality. As such, it's not to be confused with different multiple personalities. And, to some extent, it's referred to as a clone of the leader of the same ideas, beliefs, as well as values and even behaviors. This means that a pseudo is also an individual who fakes a lot of things. For instance, it could be an intellectual attempting to convince someone else that they have a great educated mind. In this case, they may not possess such greatness. A pseudo-celebrity may be an infamous individual thinking that they are prominent for doing something. In the real sense, they may not be as famous. But, having understood the traits of a pseudo personality, how can an individual get rid of it? How can you tell that you have a pseudo personality?

How to Acknowledge Your Pseudo Personality?

In this chapter, we investigate the possible explanations for the extensive development of the pseudo personality, which is also known as a cult. We also dig deep into how it forms. We investigate the doubling of the pseudo personality, its adaptation, and dissociation. We argue that this is one of the most proposed concepts of introjections. Briefly, we discuss various recovery issues regarding the proposed view of the cult-centered personality. Towards that end, we also address what it takes to acknowledge your pseudo personality. When a person is born in a family that's high-controlling by nature, it enforces a major separation from the ways of the world. Therefore, the individual develops a pseudo personality from that tender age. In many cases, they are subjected to different expectations as well as demands utilized in creating submissions coupled with conformity.

Apart from that, a person who has a pseudo personality is largely exposed to two different forms of the world. For instance, they live in the real world. But they may also be attached to the insular cultic world. This is especially common in people who have attended a public school. The two worlds, which are distinct from each other, carry various yet unique values and beliefs. On that note, it's vital to know the valid system so that you're not left confused or conflicted in any way. You will have to make a decision based on which world is safer for you. You will also need to identify key conditions that can make your life easier. That way, you will realize that no world is safer in isolation. At the same time, being a young individual who is subjected to the world of pseudo personality, you'll encounter different symptoms of depression and anxiety. The intense pressure appended to thinking as well as acting in two major ways introduces the cult identity.

The pseudo personality represses a person's original self while dissociating the defensive element in an individual. Therefore, it often allows the mind to easily cope with and then adapt to the intense demands of a group of environment. Towards that end, critical thinking, questions, in addition to feelings are squashed. In a way, the person becomes selfish and disloyal thereby entering into a certain feeling of indifference. Over the years, toxic shame becomes the norm. Dependency coupled with insecurity will then become another aspect appended to this personality disorder. It's created at your tender age as you grow. For that reason, you treat the world as your enemy. Your true self then becomes stifled to receive some form of acceptance from the community. You'll also seek love and compassion from your family. This means that your perception of yourself is largely destroyed. Shame takes over your personality.

In puberty, you become guiltier of actions that you may not be responsible for. Thereafter, you would begin to lose friends and your immediate extended family. At some point in your life, you will realize that the risk to be closed in some bud is more painful and disturbing than that of blossoming. When you reach your thirties, you'll delve into self-destruction. The people controlling you will make sure that this occurs.

In addition, children raised in different religious cults may be subjected to high expectations by the ministers and parents to submit to the various group teachings. They will also be subjected to intense pressure based on thinking and acting in two different ways that cause a cult identity. That is how the pseudo or cult personality starts to form. It represses its original self in different ways. It also dissociates the mind in coping with the contradictory, intense demands of a certain environment. As an adult, when you associate with a totalitarian group that you did not spend your younger life with, you will be encouraged to reconnect to your older self prior to joining the destructive life. Unfortunately, toddlers who have grown in an oppressive environment encounter difficulty with the pseudo personality since the kid's true self and critical thinking skills are hindered from developing.

Besides, a child raised in a harsh structure has to learn to live according to two different sets of rules: the world overview and the cult's teachings. Every element described in these worlds has some unique aspects. They both carry different values and teachings too. For that reason, the child will be left questioning the validity of every system. They may also end up being confused since the conflicting beliefs about the world pose different questions in their lives. Such children can also internalize a major point of view that the world isn't safe. Therefore, they shall become isolated within themselves. If there is any form of responding or emotional abuse coupled with trauma in the family, then the child will undoubtedly lose their self-identity.

In the past cases where an abusive group has denigrated independent thinking skills while creating dependency as well as insecurity within the personality of the child, no questions or protests were allowed by any means. In many of the abusive situations, the toddler was often made to feel that she or he was unworthy in many ways. The child, being fearful, became abnormal and mistrustful of various authority figures, including teachers and the law enforcement body. Because the same has been regarded as the enemy, such children would be unable to turn to their parents for help. As they went ahead to think as well as behave as often trained by their parents in the family structure, or better yet, the group, they stifled their initial personality while rejecting independent thoughts as selfish as well as disloyal. This had an impact on their lives such that the child's self-perception was distorted. At the same time, a framework of guilt was created in their minds. These kids ended up devaluing themselves and their feelings.

Children with strong temperaments were considered rebellious if not resistant. But such individuals may have ended up making a viably effective transition into the community following their relocation into a different environment. Part of getting to understand who they are can be as simple as finding out the basics of their personal tastes. For instance, what is an individual's personal color? What do they prefer to eat? Do they like dogs or cats? Do they prefer winter to summer? If such a person, could go anywhere across this world, where would it be? These are some of the basic elements that can assist a child survivor in understanding that there's one original self that has preferences such as likes as well as dislikes, and viewpoints.

The pseudo personality also entails a broad range of self-righteousness and a major cheating pattern in the relationship. Some may take advantage of others, as well. To fully understand the pseudo personality, we compile a list of up to 5 typical behaviors of such individuals, based on expert opinion as well as research. In this list, you'll realize that pseudo personalities have common traits. But the mentioned behaviors aren't to be used as a form of diagnosis in as much as it may give an impeccable idea regarding why someone may have a pseudo personality.

According to Psychology Today, a pseudo personality refers to a person who has a grandiosity personality disorder coupled with a lack of empathy for others. Such an individual may also need admiration from others. These traits make a pseudo personality difficult to hang out with because they are always willing to control people. Besides, they are also ruthless in manipulating people to do as they wish. To assist you in finding out if you or someone closer to you is a pseudo personality, we've created a list of alarming patterns to look at.

- Self-importance
- A belief that they are special than others
- The need for admiration on a different level
- Some sense of entitlement
- Lack of empathy
- Envy
- Arrogance

Apart from that, people with a pseudo personality can easily be affected by criticism as well as defeat. Therefore, they may easily react with disdain as well as anger. However, social withdrawal may also follow. They may also have some sense of entitlement, which may lead them to disregard other people in many ways. As a result, relationships may be damaged. Although a pseudo personality can be an overachiever, the disorder can have a negative impact on their performance. This is due to their sensitivity to criticism.

The Challenges of Dealing with a Pseudo Personality

Understanding Their Fragile Ego Could Be a Major Challenge

A person with a pseudo personality has a self-inflated ego. Such an individual is usually self-absorbed to the extent of ignoring the needs of other people. Therefore, there may be no other additional gods in their world. Even in a case where such a person says they believe in a higher being, they may not fully acknowledge the presence of God. To them, ego rules everything. When dealing with a pseudo personality, therefore, it may be challenging to identify the ego of such a person. Besides, their ego loves pleasure as well as pain.

Comprehending Their Ability to Shift Gears from the Real to the False World

The idea that someone's character can be determined by a glimpse of their face hails from the ancient era of Greece. In the 18th century, it was known as a popularized idea that was used as a talking point in the intellectual circles of psychologists. In the world of pseudoscience, a person with a pseudo personality is known for shifting gears often. Such an individual can easily shift from grandiosity to behaving like a person who is often better than the rest. You can see the pseudo personality as a person who hogs credit from the achievements of other people while milking the injured or misfortune.

At the same time, victimized pseudo personalities are constantly looking for a gullible individual that will easily believe their version of a story regardless of its realness or exaggeration. What such people claim is the fact that they have different calamities. These calamities may make them selfish and self-centered in several ways. Towards that end, you need to be aware of such personalities since they are manipulative. The moment they identify the fact that you don't share in their emotions or pamper them in a certain way that they prefer, they shall eliminate you from their lives.

The Pseudo Personality Is Pretty Controlling

The pseudo personality is known to be controlling in many ways. As such, it doesn't really destroy someone completely. It suppresses a person by dominating it. Also, it's known to want one thing at this moment and another different thing in a different moment.

All in all, the pseudo personality is programmed to lean towards wanting to quest its thirst. This is usually the opposite of the normal personality. While the real personality may be focused on wanting to get out of the abuse, the pseudo is often programmed to stay in. That's one major challenge of dealing with such a personality since it's always in control. With that said, as long as the programmed personality is in charge, you'll find it challenging to deal with a pseudo personality.

It May Be Challenging to Identify the Nitty-Gritty of a Pseudo Personality

Typically, the cult leader, who is also identified as the head of the pseudo personality, presents himself as an ideal role model in charge of the group. The individual can easily use manipulative tricks to ideally make his life and other projects successful. The rest of the team members are then led to believe that they would be happier if they lived like their leader. As a victim of such circumstances, you may find it challenging to identify such elements in a pseudo personality.

A Pseudo Personality Is a Professional Liar

A pseudo personality is a pathological liar. The individual tells lies as well as stories that may fall between delusions coupled with conscious lying. At times, they may believe their lies. Therefore, it becomes challenging to understand them, including how to deal with such issues where lies are involved. Some of these liars do it often such that even experts specializing in psychology cannot tell what's happening.

Additionally, the professionals may not even understand the difference between the facts presented at the table and fiction given after some time. Being pathological liars, such individuals tend to approach you naturally in their quest to manipulate others. Not only are they creative but also original. They are also quick thinkers such that they do not exude common signs of telling lies, including pauses and avoidance. When questioned, a pseudo personality may tell more than they have been asked without being specific regarding the question.

It May Be Difficult to Deal with Their Vicious Temper

A pseudo personality has a psychological construct that often describes a major reaction to their injury. All too often, this is conceptualized as a major threat to their self-esteem and worth. With that said, a pseudo personality is known for having a vicious temper caused by a previous interaction with someone who may have wounded them. This is the case when the individual falls from grace in that even their hidden character is revealed. It's also the case when their value, as well as importance, is questioned. A pseudo personality injury is caused by distress. It may, therefore, lead to the dysregulation of behaviors. Since they have a vicious temper as well, they may keep such traits hidden from you.

The Pseudo Personality Will Always Play a Victim

Everyone has played a victim at some point in life. In fact, some have blamed their siblings for something they may not have done. Others have even pointed the finger at a co-worker for messing up a task. While this may often be manipulative in many cases, it's also clear that people with a pseudo personality play the victim in different instances when they are guilty.

Breaking the Machination

Honestly speaking, a person with a pseudo personality is not someone you should be associating with. This is because if you'll sustain emotional as well as physical harm that you shall never recover from. With that said, you may not realize that such individuals have the mentioned traits. With it being so prevalent in the US, there are good chances that you may have encouraged many of such individuals to be in your life. Even if you didn't, chances are that you may not be in a position to spot them instantly. But, because of their potential to mask their characters, you'll find it necessary to identify specific aspects of their behavior.

Here are a few tips for breaking the machination:

Refuse to Engage with an Individual Who Has a Pseudo Personality

If you want to untangle yourself from the docket of a pseudo personality, then you can begin by refusing to associate with them. Dodge their emotional as well as physical harm that hails from dealing with them. To be more specific, the only major way to deal with them is to evade them.

Establish If the Conversation Must Always Be Spearheaded by Them

If you want to identify a pseudo personality among your friends and family, consider assessing if they always direct all conversations towards themselves. This would imply that they are not only self-centered but focused on turning every angle of discussion towards what they would rather listen to. That way, you can easily detach yourself.

Understand That They Are Takers and Not Givers Most of the Time

In the world of psychology, there are givers, takers, as well as matchers. While the givers will always find out how they can be of help to others, takers will always focus on being the recipients. On the other hand, matchers will concentrate on playing tit for tat on many occasions. In the long run, however, there's a twist to all aspects as there are instances when the givers behave like takers and vice versa. People with a pseudo personality behave like givers but end up taking everything from their loved ones if only to find comfort. That implies that if you're in a relationship with such an individual, you may end up forfeiting everything you have at the expense of the friendship or so. In the end, they will be very unwilling to give back or reciprocate in any way. To be safe while relating to such individuals, you need to be keen to observe them from a distance.

Most of these dissociative phenomena aren't necessarily as a result of symptomatic of illnesses. However, they greatly represent a continuous outset of normal psycho-biological modulation coupled with incoming information which may be stored in the long run. As such, prolonged environmental stress coupled with life situations from the usual may interfere with the integrative functions of a child's personality. People exposed to such forces may end up adapting via dissociation.

Chapter 4 – Inner Child Healing

Every person is a result of their history. In other words, you are the person you are today because of the collective experiences that have occurred in your past. Every encounter, every experience, every thought, every pain, and decisions have culminated in the creation of the person you are today. This is because of a dominant theory of development that asserts that were are products of our environments. This includes both your social and physical environments as well as your internal environment in terms of thoughts and inner experiences. The significance of these facts is to be found in the role of the environment of shaping who you are right from childhood. Psychologists believe that your formative years in childhood underpin who you become as an adult. This is because your brain is most impressionable and fragile between ages 0 to 7 years. This results in the formation of beliefs, ideas, and concepts of who you are and what you should do to gain acceptability within family, friends, and the larger society.

While these processes are largely subconscious, their significance in your life is far much more gigantic than you would like to imagine. This is because the absorbed experiences of childhood stay with you through adulthood existing only in the subconscious but manifesting in day-to-day decisions and actions. It is within the context that the concept of the inner child emerges. While a person may want to disregard this concept as another fascination of pop psychology, it is fairly easy to notice its existence in your day to day life. The inner child is largely a free spirit that loves fun, creativity, and imaginativeness. All these elements come to life at various times during your day-to-day activities. However, a lack of awareness means that it is impossible to capture its presence. For instance, when you are mindful, you can notice the inner child when you lose yourself in fun activities, enjoy a game of one kind or another or fondly reminisce on an old photo. The inner child is also evident during situations when you focus on pleasing your parents and other members of the family.

How Does It Happen?

The inner child is thus regarded as the psyche that encapsulates the qualities that you had as a child. In this case, therefore, you can consider aspects such as curiosity, spontaneity, and joyfulness that characterized your childhood. Besides the rosy and happy memories, you can also subconsciously carry the burden of a wounded past based on the traumatic and scary encounters. The negative experiences have been found to scar and wound your inner child. Leaving long-lasting impacts on how you relate and engage with your environment.

The occurrence of a wounded inner child comes about as a result of the mental and psychological underdevelopment that is unequipped to deal with the emotions and feelings associated with most challenges that defined your childhood. In other words, in the absence of appropriate cognitive abilities to comprehend the dynamics of your environment you end up with a buildup of unprocessed emotions that become a defining factor of your subconscious mind. According to psychologists, therefore, the embedded emotions become crucial markers in a person's life often causing many of the difficulties you face in your relationships, behavior, and feelings.

The suppressed emotions often become evident in your life through their behavior, relations, and activities. This because unresolved issues in your childhood are often evident through projecting roles of significant figures in your childhood on current relationships. From a psychological point of view, this occurs because you subconsciously want to resolve issues of your past by re-creating similar situations. To further appreciate this concept, you can consider the example of a person who has unresolved issues with his or her father, and as such he or she will project these feelings to their boss or any other authority figure. Suppressed emotions can also manifest in your life through numerous mental disorders including identity problems, low self-esteem, psychosexual difficulties as well as criminal behavior. Additionally, you may also notice instances of lack of belief and trust in yourself and others, the development of various addictions, and the lack of genuine friends in your life.

While these examples do not cover the entirety of aspects of a wounded inner child, they do offer crucial insights into how failing to address the inner child can directly affect the quality of your life. By appreciating the impact of unresolved and suppressed emotions in your life as well as the presence of your inner child, you are initiating a process of transformation like no other. Unlike the love and care you may show towards your child, pet, friend, or family member, acknowledging your inner child creates space for the onset of a transformational experience like no other. The liberation of your mind from the numerous mental and emotional burdens that define your current life lies in the ability to embrace your inner child. This is then followed by a deliberate and conscious effort of initiating a healing process that will see you become whole again.

The contact process is, therefore vital in the sense that it makes it possible for you to reinitiate the severed link to your inner child. As abstract as this may seem, your complete belief in this process offers unprecedented benefits for your current and future life. Contact is made through an objective reflective process that is designed to help you come to terms with the onset of your phase of pain life. Visualization is the most suitable in this regard. It involves picturing yourself as a child from as far back as you can remember and exploring the happy, sad, scary or joyful moments that formed part of your childhood. Patience and quite are vital in the attainment of this goal owing to the fact that they make it possible for your brain to uncover the hidden emotions and experienced that characterized your upbringing. This process can take up to an hour or longer and should be done comprehensively to ensure that all perspectives have been brought to light.

In encountering some of the residual pain and negativity of your childhood experience, the feeling of hate is likely to arise. However, your focus should be on uncovering the underlying emotions rather than reacting to them. This will mean maintaining a sense of compassion and understanding for yourself and those that might have inflicted the pain. By understanding and validating the pain to wash over your body, you are primarily taking charge of an experience that you had locked out for years. It is at this point that you must talk to your inner child. While this is pure imagination and visualization, it does help your subconscious mind to reveal some of the underlying challenges and how they continue to hamper your life. Creating space for communication and conversation with your inner child makes it possible for the adult brain to process past experiences and pain for better outcomes.

The process of introspection as an adult makes it possible for proper organization and cohesiveness in your narrative of life. With the capacities attained by your adult mind, the brain is able to reframe your childhood experiences with the realization that your tormentors might have been victims of abuse as well. The change of perspective goes a long way in helping you reconnect your body, mind, and soul. The sensations and feelings that have been suppressed for years often create a gap of emotional experiences. As an adult, this gap can cause a crisis of identity that is manifested in various maladaptive behaviors and tendencies. The reconnection process is thus used to integrate the new processed story into your subconscious mind.

The reconnection process is the culmination of your healing journey in that it allows your cells, consciousness, and soul to embody a new and coherent narrative that has been formed out of logical process, compassion, and forgiveness. This process should then be cemented through the process of consolation. The consolation process involves the commitment to upholding the reestablished relationship. As you begin to become aware of the outer environment, your imagination must focus on reminding the inner child of the continued relationship that will ensue from the reconciliation process. This means, the care and attention necessary to nurture the inner child will continue into the future.

The Inner Child in Adulthood

It is important that you are awakening to the fact that the existence of the inner child is an inherent part of your life. The fact that your once were a child means that you still embody the memories and experiences of this period of your life, though unconsciously. The unappreciated fact of life is that many of the so-called adults have their age as the core factor of their adulthood, but psychologically, they remain insecure and oblivious of who they really are. True maturity is defined by your ability to take responsibility for nurturing your inner child with the care and attention that characterizes any effective parenting process. In the absence of proper care and attention, as is the case with neglect and suppress that characterizes most adult reactions to the inner child, subtle symptoms emerge.

Your inner child encapsulates the innocence, wonder, joy, and sensitivity that defines childhood experiences. Additionally, the inner child is also made up of the fears and traumas that might have defined your upbringing. By rejecting or denying your inner child you not only do you eliminate the positive qualities and potential the inner children represent but that you also wrongly assume that you have outgrown your negative childhood experiences. As a result, while you might regard yourself as mature, at the core of your being you still harbor your little self, though unconsciously. In essence, most of your decisions emanate from a fearful and highly traumatized child despite the so-called adulthood you have gained through the passage of time.

The challenge for many adults as has been pointed out time and again, the absence of awareness of the inner child. This unconsciousness facilitates the subtle intrusion of the disenchanted inner child in day-to-day decisions and behaviors. For adults, therefore, the first step of peacefully coexisting with your inner child involves becoming conscious that your younger self is still very much a part of you as are your soul and mind. With this acknowledgment, a psychological adult must take the time to appreciate the message and significance of their inner child. In other words, while you might agree with this concept, intellectually, its impact in your life will only manifest once you begin to take your inner child seriously.

Guided by the primal needs that define childhood, such as love, protection, and understanding, you must then begin to communicate and engage with your inner child. The mark of adulthood is, therefore, in accordance with the willingness to become aware of the insufficiencies of childhood as well as the time and effort that is necessary to transmute these shortcomings. The gist of adulthood is that it comes with experience and capacity of logical thinking. As a result, this means that your adult personality can easily learn and adopt new skills. In this regard, you are at liberty to establish a new relationship with your inner child based on compassion and understanding. As it the case with parenting a flesh-and-blood child, you must assume a similar stance in approaching your inner child. This means developing boundaries, organized structures as well as the necessary disciplines to guide behavioral tendencies. Such an approach ultimately results in a cooperative and mutually beneficial relationship between your inner child and your adult self.

What Does a Stable Childhood Look Like?

It is pointless to discuss the process of healing your inner child without looking at some of the defining factors that make up a stable childhood. In other words, without understanding what you may have missed in your upbringing, it may be impossible to pinpoint the exact wounds you may have accumulated during your childhood. The overarching concept about a stable childhood involves the freedom of exploration, the safety, and security of guardianship as well as the attention and care for your fragile soul and mind. In other words, your childhood should comprise an understanding of family, supportive friends and relatives, and most importantly, a safe and ordered society. These three tenets underpin the basic dynamics of a stable childhood experience.

At the family level, you learn about freedom, independence, love, and attention. The home environment should be a safe space in which you are fully protected, cared for, and appreciated. With imagination and creativity bubbling through your mind as a child, you also require time to play and explore various limits of your abilities. This proves vital in helping you identify your interests and strengths as well as weaknesses. A child must also learn the importance of teamwork, sharing, and respect. These values are largely adopted during group play with other children. The freedom to venture beyond the walls of the house is thus a vital tenet of a stable upbringing. As the child is exposed to perspectives that they are different from their own, not only do they gain new perspectives but that they begin to understand who they are and what they stand for.

Rules, structure, and organization are also essential for your childhood. With limited cognitive capacities as a child, you often lack the capacity to analyze and appreciate the gravity of various experiences and encounters. It is for this reason that the family social environment must offer some sort of order and structure. The discipline and structures adopted within the family and large social circle prove vital in helping children appreciate the importance of standing up for something worthwhile. Besides enjoying loads of fun, children also need to feel loved and cared for. Parents and guardians must be willing to create time for their children in which the child is the main focus of attention. Dotting on your child allows them to integrate the fact that they are loved and that they can always have somewhere to run to in cases of trouble. While seemingly insignificant, these tenets define who you are as an adult since they are embedded deep inside your subconscious mind.

Caring for Your Inner Child

The purpose of understanding your inner child in adulthood, as well as the definition of a stable childhood, is to help you come to terms with the fact that you could be harboring a wounded inner child while remaining unawares. Once you have established this as a fact, the healing process can be initiated, as has been stipulated before. You have to understand that just as it is challenging to nurture and raise a child, so will the process of healing your inner child. Patience, commitment and determination are three vital ingredients that will help you emerge from the pool of mad that you have been downing in all your life. It is important to note that upon healing old would, you must assume the duty and responsibility of caring for your inner child. Neglect and denial offer no meaningful solutions, and as such, in the absence of sustained care, you may develop abandon your inner child and continue to suppression of emotions.

Identifying Childhood Pain

The identification of the root cause of your pain is the very beginning of a life-transforming journey. The willingness and commitment to transmute your pain into meaningful and progressive energy must start at the point of origin. As had been pointed out earlier, visualization is a vital tenet in this particular effort, more importantly, however, is the need for the meditation. By consciously exploring the depths of your mind subconscious with a focus on childhood experience, you encounter some of the joyous and painful experiences of your past. It is within this particular context that you will come face to face with pain and hurt that defined your upbringing.

Re-Parenting Your Inner Child

As is the case with your child, sibling, or relative, guidance, care, and attention underpin the process of healing the inner child. In other words, you must be ready to undertake the slow and gradual process of letting yourself come to terms with your past. This will allow you to reestablish safe and healthy ties with your inner child. As an adult, you must undertake this process, realizing that your mental, physical, and psychological health hinge upon the success of this particular endeavor. While professional help is often encouraged when it comes to establishing new ties with your inner child, the process can be achieved single-handedly by adopting approaches that define the nurturing of an actual child.

The re-parenting process is, therefore, dotted with affirmations that remind you of your true values and ideals as well as self-talks that serve to address various issues and challenges that arise in day-to-day experiences. As is the case with taking care of a child, you must also offer yourself rewards for achievements and improvements arising from the commitment of newer and stronger relations. Finally, a sense of mindfulness underpins the re-parenting process. Staying aware of the experiences and encounters of the present is vital in reconciling your past and present. This eliminates the psychological dissonance that might arise subconsciously and thus influence your decisions and behavior.

Engaging Your Inner Child

Listening and talking to your inner child are some of the effective ways of engaging with who you were as a child and how you can relate as a better human being. Engagement efforts encompass activities such as listening and talking to your inner child or more detailed methods such as writing to yourself. Talking and listening to yourself helps you come to terms with the needs of your inner child. It is with this information that you will be able to initiate meaningful changes in your behavior to make it possible for the inner child to thrive. Engagement with your inner child must focus on the original fears and issues that might have been present in your childhood. More importantly, however, to guide the inner child to the present. In other words, the talk should focus on helping the inner child appreciate the transformations that have since arisen and how the past has shaped who you are as a person in the present.

Chapter 5: Creating Your Thoughts

Thinking availability is very vital when it comes to developing your reality. Anything that you will think of in the physical world will have some clues from the inside world of your thinking and perceptions. You can be the boss of your intention when you control the thoughts you have and their dominance. When you do that, then then you will experience in knowing the truth behind your thinking and how you come up with authenticity. A lot of people always take it that they can't have control over what they are thinking. You can find yourself having flowing thoughts in your mind that are brought about by invisible force. You are advised not to have mercy with your inner thoughts as they will stem your ego and bring about insignificant issues. When you get to know how to control your dreams, then this will bring about the enacting of what you want and feel is the best.

Awareness

The first thing for you to do in having control over your views is by identifying undesirable patterns. Unless you are sure of determining the negative impacts in your thoughts, then you won't be able to come up with the positive effects. You can look up to you as if you are assessing some activities. Get back deep in your mind and listen to your inner mockery and try to determine whether it's a hurdle to your capability to have fun in life when you hear your thoughts can be the first practice because you are well conversant with your inner voice that comes along with your character due to the background distractions.

Occasionally, you will be able to identify some detailed thoughts more so when you hold on your activities for a period and pause. Nevertheless, most of the time of your life is spent in action and not being thus making you an autopilot and making you engrossed in involvement with full consciousness. Being an autopilot, you are still able to influence your feelings by your opinions despite being not attentive to their presence. With this, your inner voice will insistently notify you that life is negative; thus, you will have negativity in your focus. Your knowledge will bring out uncertainties that shoot from cynical intellectuals.

Hearing of the Inner Voice

You are advised to learn how to listen to your inner voice when you are alone and try to know what is going through your brain. You will get to know that as you wait for your thoughts, and this may often be occurring when your inner voice goes silent. With this, then there will be some discovery on the spaces amid your thoughts where peace and healing can come from. When there is an appearance of ideas, you are advised not to give any judgment about them, thus offer them some moments to develop then pay attention. Try to find out whether your inner voice is critical or expressing distress. You can still get to know whether your thoughts are positive and have appreciation and indebtedness.

Negative and positive thinking

When you think of appreciating, then you will be able to make up happiness and bring forth greater joy to your life. When they are formed in your brain, then you have to amplify them and bring them to your heart, where they will have a sharp point. When you have negative thoughts, then you will likely be advised to soothe your inner being by compassion. Don't let yourself be mad anytime you feel your inner part is not the way you want it to be. Perhaps you are supposed to send a feeling of love from your heart and make the negativity inside you billow away as you keep your focus on positive subjects.

5 Steps to Regain Control of Your Thoughts

Thoughts are considered to be either our worst friends or enemies, and this is according to a Buddhist monk Matthieu Ricard. At least every individual has had a moment when their minds have minds of their own, but still controlling their thoughts, thus enhancing happiness, reduced stress and well equipped in problem solving and achieving of goals. A lot of individuals are not always informed of what they are thinking about.

Similarly, you will be your observer and controller on the impacts that your thoughts will have on yourself. You may find yourself being depressed, mad, frustrated, sad, among others. Some simple steps help you in controlling your thoughts and stopping negative thinking.

1. Study How to Prevent Your Thoughts

You have to learn how-to put-on hold when you are in the middle of your dreams. It may be a dull, harmful, or useful idea. Most of the time during the day, you will get yourself thinking. When you feel frustrated, mad, or tired about certain things, you will have some tendency of still pressing on in whatever feeling you have; thus, this isn't an advisable approach. You will become more stupid when you trend to be angrier and more emotional. You can quickly note such in others and not in yourself. In cases where you have kids, then try to think of how your kids become stupid when they get mad an irritated. When you have no kids, then you can use a friend's. You can also have another option of thinking about that lady or man around you that is temperamental. Think deeply about your thoughts before pressing on for five minutes.

2. Recognize Negative Feelings Within You

When you can stop your beliefs, then this will assist you with times ahead. You can fast evaluate yourself on how you are feeling then get backward. Every feeling you are having is directly the outcome of something you were thinking. For instance, you can question yourself why you are anxious by taking some steps back when you have a feeling of being anxious. You may be having a project or going to fire somebody; thus, you have to know what is making you anxious. Think of what is making you worried if you had a bad experience, among many other questions. Just try to get the main problem of your anxiety. In any case, know that whatever is making you anxious will be the reason your brain is using in creating an emotional mood. Though at times, it's not the primary cause of your emotional state.

3. Note down Your Mental Tape

With the previous step correctly done, then you are capable of recognizing the movie that is in your mind. This can be a meeting that your boss chewed on you. It can also be the time when you flopped during a presentation. You can also be disturbed by the voice of your dad, telling you how worthless you are. A lot of people have negative mental tapes that bring about negativity canceling positive tapes. There is a time where current situations will make you replay the previous status of that movie. You can have five successful occurrences, and one disappointment and your mind will want to get to the frustration because of the need to avoid pain than seek pleasure. All you are required to do is identify the content of the tape then note it down. This will help you get it out of your mind.

Writing it down will get it outside your brain, and you will have distanced yourself from sentiments that it makes. This can be referred to as dissociation and when you note down your mental tapes is part of it. You will find it very simple because you need a pen and a paper. When you dissociate yourself from something, then it's like you have excluded yourself from the first-person spot in the brain. If you are to be asked about a painful experience in the past to think about like it's happening, then you will be able to take yourself back to that condition. This can cheer up feelings, thus making you angry, sad, among many other emotions. This can be known as associates. You are placing yourself in an event. In most default occasions, the mental tapes play like this and take us back to the situation of pain. When you note down your mental tapes that it will remove you from the point of associating with anxiety, giving you some step to move out of the situation. This step will be a positive step in helping you calm down. When you remove the tapes from your mind, it will also remove their power.

4. Get the Lie

In every mental tape, there is a lie about yourself on what you are choosing to believe, whether deliberately or subconsciously. You should be able to find what the myth is, and this a significant step. The lie can be that you are a nobody, or a failure in life, amongst many other things. You can some experience as someone told you no woman would love you. You have to inscribe it in your mental tape fast.

5. Find the Truth

You will want to combat the myth; thus, the only solution is to find out the truth about yourself. You can be in prayers, reading your Bible, and trying to inquire from God what He destined you to be. There are different processes you can use. You can decide to talk to friends about it or seek advice from your coach. It doesn't matter the route you will take as long as you get to the truth. When you find the truth, then you can write it next to the lie. Put it in the first person and phrase it positively. Instead of that noting it down like "you are not a failure," you can phrase it, "you are a better individual full of positive impacts." Even the Bible talks about in Philippians 4:8.

Get Rid of The Poor Self-Concept of Your Thoughts

Seeing yourself unworthy, incompetent, failure can't be known as having low self-esteem. Such opinions will bring about the creation of negative thoughts that can easily affect your life decisions, thus decreasing your esteem. You can decide to use some tools of mindfulness as you study other situations without having a negative influence on your past.

Live in the Moment

With a good focus on time, then you will likely have to select your moves wisely and precisely. This will be done without having any effects of your past, not considering any worries but having positives hopes about the future.

Create Awareness

When you are aware, then you will quickly recognize how you are reacting and tackling your uncertainties, making a moment amid your feelings and activities. You are then expected to answer a healthier way.

Inscribe in a Journal

A lot of your views and feelings have been locked in your hidden mind, and inscribing can assist you in bringing them into your alertness. When you write what you feel and think can help you to sort negative concepts about yourself from the truth of who you are in reality.

Don't Judge

Approaching your life without judging will make you accept yourself, your involvements, disappointments, and achievements, and what people say about you without being worried if it's good or bad or you have self-importance or disgrace.

Be Connected to Yourself

When you are mindful, then it can assist you to enhance a sense of fitting together to yourself and reduce the people you want to please by making you put on hold autopilot thinking and characters that will make you want to satisfy individuals and forgetting about your wants.

Enhance Watchful Meditation

When you are meditating, it merely means you are letting go of the competing thoughts that are in your concentration and tolerating that those feelings and beliefs are temporary rather than parts of yourself. You are supposed to preserve some moments daily to be still and focus on conscious and watch your worries billow away like clouds.

Have Participation in Your Personal Life

Mindfulness inspires us to become lively and confident in enhancing your own experiences. When you are aware of your thoughts and selecting your replies will permit you to act and take part in your personal lives.

Advanced Beginner's Mind

With a beginner's mind, you will look at things like you are sighting them for the first time with a lot of sincerity, enthusiasm, and liberty from anticipation. You will see things in a new light rather than robotically retorting with the old patterns of character.

Let Go

The goal of being mindfulness is by either non-attachment or letting go. Letting go of what you are thinking of or what you should do, you can be able to have trust in yourself and decide on what you feel is right for you.

Have Compassion to Yourself

You are supposed to have love towards yourself as much as anyone else. When you have self-compassion, then you will be able to give yourself love, protection, and reception you want.

Refocus Your Mind

Having a wandering brain will be beneficial and has become achievable. When you are enhancing your mental focus, which is attainable, that won't mean that it will be fast and straightforward. If it would have been easy, then all of us would require a very sharp attentiveness. Some ideas can help you enhance your mental focus and attentiveness.

Begin by Assessing your Mental Focus

You have to know the strength of your mental focus before you begin working on enhancing your mental focus. Your focus will be great if you find it simple to be alert, set goals and try breaking your tasks to smaller parts, and take short rests and get back to work. Your focus should be worked on if you are regularly daydreaming, can't point out obstacles, and quickly lose your level of progress. With more learning, then you probably have an excellent attention ability if your statements are like your style. If your focus has to be worked on, then you will have to be so strict on your mental focus enhancement. This can take much time, but with learning good habits and being stable in your mind, then you can be assisted.

Eradicate Interferences

You have to accept that you saw this phrase coming. It can be healthy, but many people have underestimated how so many interferences have hindered them from being attentive to the tasks they have at hand. Such distractions can come from loud music from the background. Controlling such disturbances can be more relaxed, but still, there are some challenges you are supposed to handle. A simple way of dealing with such is by just excusing yourself and requesting to be left alone for some time and getting some specific time just for yourself. You can also go somewhere that you won't have any distractions and work peacefully. Places like libraries, your house, or a silent coffee shop can be good joints to give a try. You may try to rest before handling any task to help you to fight off anxiety and worry; thus, you will need the use of positive thoughts. In situations where your mind has focused on distracting things, then you have to bring it back to the work that you have at hand.

Put Your Focus on One Thing at a Time

When having several tasks at hand, you will tend to work out fast to finish; thus, this may lead to having the functions poorly done. Doing so many works at once will decrease your productivity, thus making you leave out some essential ideas out. Take your focus like a spotlight that you shine it at a particular area, you have clear visibility, unlike when you cross it in a dark room where you won't have a clear vision. To improve your focus, all you can do is enhancing the resources you have. Just stop doing so many things at once and focus on one task at a time.

Be in the Moment

You may find it tiresome to be focused mentally when you are still thinking of the past due to other reasons. At some point, you have been able to encounter people talk about being present. This when you are supposed to put away all the distractions and fully concentrate mentally on the current moment. The notion of staying present is vital for recollecting your mental focus. When you are fully engaged, then you will be attentive and get the essential points at that particular time. You may take some duration to study how to be at the moment. You are not able to change what occurred in the past, and the future has not happened yet; thus, what you do currently will assist you to avoid your past errors and make way for a great future.

Exercise Mindfulness

This an important topic to talk about and for good reasons. A lot of people studied how to be mindful for many years and its health benefits, but it has just started to be understood recently. There is a study where professionals engaged humans to assist in sort complex doing of many tasks in a day. The jobs had to be done within 20 minutes, which includes picking up calls, planning meetings, among many other tasks. When you are training about mindfulness, then you will involve yourself on how to deliberate. You might consider the job to be simple, but it's more complicated than it appears. With time you will get to know that it's easier to bring your focus to where it is supposed to be.

Take a Small Break

You have probably been in a situation where you are doing a task for a long time, and then your focus breaks down with time; thus, you will be in a problematic condition trying to bring back your mental focus to the task at hand. This will significantly affect your performance too. It is advisable that anytime you have an elongated responsibility, try and give yourself some short break. Try shifting your attention to something different just for a duration. The breaks will provide you with a sharp mental focus, and you will have a high-performance impact on your task.

Practice More to Strengthen Your Focus

The building your mental focus is something that won't take a short period, but it has so many steps to go through. Sports professionals also need time to practice and help in firming their intent skills. You will note your impact when you first try to recognize that distraction will affect your life. When you find yourself being detailed by other unimportant issues, you have to focus more on giving yourself time. When you enhance your focus, then you will be able to achieve so many things in life like success, happiness, and fulfillment.

Tips for Improving Mindfulness

Some techniques can help in enhancing awareness of the current moment, such as:

1. Just Respire

When you are seated, try being mindful of your breath. Try and concentrate on how the belly is rising, thus will make you focus and be aware. Try and focus on your breathing when you are waiting for a bus, when in a traffic jam when waiting to eat, among others. When you have a single breath purposefully, then this can be a great way to enhance mindfulness.

2. Have a Walk

You have to get up and have a walk with purpose and awareness. Get somewhere attractive where you can go and walk and get to spend any minute of knowledge. Try looking at the muscles in your legs and toes as they move and carry your body. You can try to make walking meditation your day to day routine.

3. Enjoy Being in Silence

The best condition for achieving mindfulness is quiet. Teach yourself to enact it and explore it. Your life is always calm, but you still get some distractions that fill that void like music, a ring of a phone, traffic sounds, and airplanes above. You have to be silent and try to explore during that time. Try to get to understand feelings of anxiety that often arise and making you forgo your distractions.

How to Affirm Yourself

1. Remove Selfish and Cynical Individuals in Your Life

The first is staying from individuals with negativity and those who will bring stress and sadness to your life. You are advised not to cut them from your life completely. This is understandable because it can be impossible. You have to avoid making them your priorities and get to them when you are right to do so. You will find it very difficult to have confidence in the people who treated you badly and never appreciated you. When you are choosing your friends, upgrade your standards.

2. Have Goals and Achieve Them

You have to get some breakthroughs before you reach specific points on enhancing the quality of your life. Your goals don't matter whether they are big or small as long as you achieve them. There is a level you will realize your efforts are paying off and bringing you nearer to your desires. Always try improving different categories in your life, thus bringing more improvement.

3. Expand Yourself

One of the most significant hurdles that one faces in having confidence is being unemployed. When you are not employed, you will have financial strains and a lot of issues to handle. Instead of having some sympathy for yourself about being jobless, try taking your time to enhance yourself and information and aids. Just evaluate yourself and try to get what you are interested in and get some good time with the people you love. Make sure you can create connections that can be positively great in giving you opportunities.

4. Have Time to Assist Others

When you do positive things to others, then it will bring a positive impact on yourself. You will have to realize that making someone happy will help in enhancing the life of someone and inspiring others. When you affirm yourself, it's just not about you but trying to be kind and helpful to others. These ideas will be useful in enhancing yourself.

Chapter 6: Survival Mode

So, you have found yourself as a victim of a severe narcissist; whether domestic, parental, or work-related, walking away is a viable option. Other people may not understand why you did it, but without the deep insight into your partner, how could they?

It may trouble you trying to understand why your partner did the things they did and how they did them. Don't they care about the relationship? Don't they care about you? These are common thoughts that may cross your mind like a broken record. When you find that you are consumed with these negative, sad thoughts, remind yourself that it is possible to forget and live on- stronger and smarter.

Is it PTSD?

Victims of narcissistic abuse exhibit psychological symptoms of post-traumatic stress disorder (PTSD). Unlike PTSD that can be caused by a single traumatic event, narcissistic trauma is under a separate clinical term for severe, repetitive, prolonged trauma-complex PTSD, or C-PTSD. The survivors appear to be disconnected and unaware of their emotional anguish and pain-ridden thoughts. When the victim of abuse can receive validation of the reality of their experience, the cognitive dissonance abates and dissolves.

Complex PTSD usually involves emotional or physical torture; for example, childhood trauma, domestic violence, or even sexual abuse. Because the abuser forms a biochemical bond with his/her victim, it becomes exceedingly challenging to detach yourself from them. However, that does not mean that suffering is not real or severe. Unfortunately, there have been instances where a victim of covert emotional abuse is driven to commit suicide. Society is uncertain of how to deal with the narcissist partners and survivors.

The abuser struggles to demonstrate the absurdity of the victim's reality claims. This sort of psychological warfare takes on a lasting effect on the survivor's brain due to chronic psychological trauma. There is often a lot of breaking up and making up in the course of the relationship because the narcissist does not seek help, and neither does the survivor. The survivor may fail to report the abuse because of fear of the unknown. They risk being believed and understood by society. Also, survivors struggle with protecting their self-worth and protecting their abusers.

How Can You Tell if You Have C-PTSD?

Often victims of narcissistic abuse experience self-worthlessness and seek to correct their characteristic flaws pointed out by the abuser. Persons suffering from this type of abuse are often obsessed with their shortcomings and failures in the relationship; not as they have experienced but as the abuser has outlined them. Their thoughts are regularly beating them up and self-condemning. They may say, "It's my fault really," "I cannot blame him for yelling at me," "I am the reason she is having an affair." It is common for them to beat themselves up for the actions of their abusers.

Narcissistic abuse survivors suffer symptoms to include:

Intrusive depressing thoughts

The intrusive thoughts may manifest in terms of memories of traumatic events, nightmares, and upsetting dreams containing aspects of the traumatic episodes. Other times they may occur as flashbacks that may lead to loss of consciousness and increased physiological effects such as rapid heart rate after exposure to triggers.

Stress

Exposure to trauma can lead the victim to cause serious injury to themselves or others, commit suicide, or project sexual violence to others. Other direct witnesses to these circumstances may also succumb to stress factors.

Avoidance

People who have been through troubling series of events are prone to avoid reminders of the trauma. They tend to keep away from external reminders such as people, places, activities, and even conversations. They also block thoughts that may remind them of the trauma they suffered.

Exclusion

Survivors tend to detach and isolate themselves from close friends and relatives and social activities. Dissociation is expected from a victim of trauma as it is the mind's way of recovering.

Changes in Arousal and Reactivity

The trauma triggers may worsen after the victim has detached from the abuser and abusive situations. For example, the survivor may become more irritable or aggressive, easily alarmed, and hyperattentive. They may also exhibit trouble concentrating and sleeping, as well as show some self-destructive behavior.

Difficulty Controlling Emotions

You may experience difficulty in controlling your negative thoughts and feelings, such as depression, anger, and irritability.

Altered Perception of Self and World

The victim's entire existence is shaped by the abuser. They rewrite their previous beliefs about themselves and the world to the views of their abuser. Their self-worthlessness is drilled into them, and so their self-image becomes distorted. They experience feelings of helplessness, guilt, and shame. They view the world and themselves negatively.

Obsession with the Abuser

The survivors may develop an unhealthy obsession with their abusers. They become codependent- like one another's drug. You put your emotional, psychological and physical health aside to appease your abuser. The obsession may go as far as the victim plotting revenge against the abuser. They become consumed with their abuser and let the feelings they elicit foster.

Difficulty with Personal Relationships

You may experience trouble forging friendships or relationships outside the abuser. For example, your current relationships may disintegrate because of your exclusion, and you may find it difficult to interact with other people owing to your new perception of yourself and the world around you.

Studies have shown that survivors of this kind of trauma suffer what is called mental death because they have been victimized so long that they lose their pre-trauma identity.

Anyone can develop post-traumatic stress disorder- at any age. The risk factors that increase the risk of PTSD include:
- Holidays and anniversaries
- Getting hurt or seeing another person hurt
- Feeling helplessness or horror
- Stress

- Little or no social support
- Childhood trauma, and
- History of mental illness or substance abuse

In addition to these symptoms, it may be common to feel like you are not ready to forgive. Do not rush yourself into recovery. You will need to relearn most of the emotions and emotional cues, such as:

- Hope
- Trust
- Limits and boundaries
- Regaining your life
- Gratitude and happiness
- Rebuilding friendships and
- Self-love

Getting Help

If you have PTSD from a complicated relationship, it is necessary to seek validation of your experiences to heal. Keeping a journal is an excellent way to keep track of your emotions, as well as any other physical and psychological changes to your body.

Deteriorating C-PTSD symptoms can lead to a decline in your quality of life. If you experience these symptoms for longer than four weeks, you must seek professional help. If gone untreated, patients find unhealthy, destructive coping habits like substance abuse. It is not necessarily true that time heals all wounds. Seeking professional help ensures that a proper physical and psychological evaluation is conducted to eliminate any symptoms caused by pre-existing conditions. A proper evaluation also aims to define your symptoms for correct diagnosis.

Recovery from abuse needs the integration of the cognitive, psychological, and emotional parts of the brain. Three necessary conditions are; maintaining a safe space meaning a trauma-free zone, the recollection of the circumstances and mourning the past, and lastly, reconnection with your new life.

Some resilience factors that may minimize the risk of suffering PTSD include:

Finding a Support Group

Finding support works as a safety plan to help you deal with stressful situations. It is an excellent strategy to plan ahead in case you are confronted with a psychologically draining circumstance. Make a list of emergency contacts whom you can dial should you feel the need.

Identify Early Warning Triggers

Warning signs often precede symptoms. Anticipating warning signs and triggers such as negative thoughts, change in mood, and behavior can help you learn how to manage them better to avoid PTSD relapse as you heal. For example, you may be triggered by hearing a frustrated someone shouting at a person, or a pet, or even a machine. Other external triggers, such as hearing a song that marks a traumatic stage in your life. Mental preparation to deal with unforeseen triggers eliminates panic and helps you cope easier.

Identify Coping Methods

Once you have identified the internal and external warning signs, it is time to whip out your most preferred coping method for that particular trigger. For example, you can write several step-by-step coping cards that you can carry with you in case of anything. Let's say you hear that song that reminds you of dark times, calmly retrieve your cards and see which coping strategy works best to relax you. There are also a variety of software applications that can help cater to stress and anxiety management.

Recovery is best done with the right combination of clinical, family, and peer support. Helping a C-PTSD survivor goes beyond PTSD treatment into assisting them to regain power, self-control, and self-identity. C-PTSD is not yet well recognized by medical practitioners, as it needs to be diagnosed and treated differently from other mental disorders and PTSD. Its treatment focuses mainly on therapy; standard behavioral therapies, and exposure therapies. Medication is also prescribed for extreme cases.

Psychotherapy

In the confines of a safe space, a clinician or therapist will encourage you to talk about the trauma you experienced. This form of therapy is conducted either on a one-on-one basis or as group treatment. To achieve a well-rounded treatment, the therapist may combine different types of approaches depending on your individual needs, be it focusing on the symptoms or concentrate on your social life; family, work, and relationships.

Psychotherapy takes about 7 to 14 weeks, where the patient gradually learns to trust the therapist; and the therapist, in turn, helps the patient identify his/her symptoms and triggers, as well as develop healthy coping mechanisms. Psychotherapy helps the patient learn
- about trauma and its effects
- how to relax in high-stress situations
- tips and tricks to a healthy lifestyle and sleep patterns
- how to deal with emotions of shame, guilt, and helplessness, among others.

Cognitive-Behavioral Therapy

This is one example of therapy treatments that help the patients to remain mindful of their moods and bodily sensations and how to deal with them as they arise. This type of therapy also educates the family members of the patient on how to recognize and deal with a C-PTSD survivor.

Exposure therapy is a form of CBT that involves gradually exposing yourself to already experienced trauma but in a safe "controlled" environment. The patient may revisit these traumas by way of visualizing, writing or visiting places where the trauma occurred. This strategy helps the survivors face their fears and overcome them.

Cognitive restructuring therapy pairs well with exposure therapy. Often victims of trauma link people, places, things, and events with negative thoughts. Cognitive restructuring helps them healthily rewrite these thoughts by replacing the negative thoughts about these places with a more objective one. With the help of the therapist, patients can take another rational look at situations and free themselves of pent-up emotions about it.

Eye movement desensitization and reprocessing (EMDR) therapy involves some factors of psychotherapy that is used to relieve traumatic triggers in small doses as the therapist directs your eye movement with rhythmic right-left stimulation. By diverting your attention while recollecting traumatic events, you are prone to have reduced psychological reactions to these memories. With time, the disturbing memories will have little to no impact on you. Multiple studies have shown that EMDR is useful in treating PTSD and other mental conditions such as depression, stress, anxiety, eating disorders, and addictions.

Medications

Although there are no medications that are C-PTSD approved, some medicines are prescribed together with psychotherapy to alleviate the symptoms, but they do not treat the disorder. Antidepressants are a conventional treatment for PTSD symptoms. The patients should remain honest in the subjective diagnosis for the doctor to arrive at the best combination of medication for them. A combination of antipsychotics, antidepressants, and anti-anxiety medication helps the patient manage C-PTSD symptoms or recurrent disorders that may arise because of or alongside it.

Along with treatment, it is beneficial also to help yourself. It is understandably difficult to take that first step into recovery, but it is the most vital step. Take care of yourself and expect your symptoms to improve over time. Engaging in physical activity is an excellent way to get moving. Exercises release feel-good hormones that help you relax. You could also immerse yourself in comforting social situations, you may feel uneasy at first, but it gradually gets better and more comfortable. Try to confide in a close family member or friend.

Gratitude Exercises

"Gratitude drives happiness. Happiness boosts productivity. Productivity unveils mastery. And, mastery motivates the world." - Robin Sharma

Exercising gratitude is a powerful human emotion. Gratitude occurs in many forms; you could be thanking The Almighty, Mother Nature, yourself, whomever. Thankfulness comes easy to survivors of trauma, and exercising it for even a short period can cause a notable improvement in your health and life.

Trauma causes psychopathological conditions and strips away your happiness. The relationship between gratitude and joy is multifaceted. Although happiness is found to be a genetic factor- in that people tend to fall back to a particular level of happiness, through gratitude exercises, it can be improved. For example, you could send a thank you note to your close friend or family member for their constant support. You will find that this act of kindness will considerably improve your mood.

Gratitude exercises not only increase your level of happiness but also improves health. Studies have shown a notable connection between gratitude and good psychological and physical health. "Positive psychology" research shows that cultivating positive thoughts, habits, and beliefs may equally impact post-trauma symptoms like stress.

In addition to happiness, gratitude restores your former level of functioning. For example, if your work has been suffering due to C-PTSD, you could return to your productive kick-ass self by perhaps keeping a gratitude journal. Grateful employees are more productive, efficient, and more responsible. Employees who express gratitude create a sense of camaraderie in the company's productivity.

While anxiety is a useful mechanism that the body uses to alert you of lurking danger and deployment of the fight or flight responses, it becomes harmful when it is unbridled. By a conscious effort to exercise gratitude, you retrain the brain to select only the positive images, and outcomes hence reduce anxiety. A study conducted with a large group of men showed that a grateful outlook on life allows us to gain acceptance without fear of the future. Gratitude exercises are especially useful in treating phobias.

As a trauma survivor, make a conscious effort to set aside some time every day to express gratitude. Perhaps you are grateful from time-to-time, but setting daily reminders goes a long way into cultivating positive thoughts and habits. Being thankful every day helps you cope better with traumatic memories.

Here are small exercises to help you cultivate joy and happiness:

Compliments to myself	People I am grateful for
Current assets	Current challenges

Appreciate Yourself

Self-appreciation improves mood. Look at yourself in the mirror and shower yourself with compliments on your current efforts, past achievements, skills or abilities, and virtues. You may also include your physique- be thankful for your chiseled nose, your long neck, etc. Use positive words like brave, strong, beautiful, and the like. Notice that your mood gets better with every adjective.

Keep a Gratitude Journal

Psychotherapists highly recommend expressive writing. Make your gratitude journal personal. You may prefer to write long journal entries or just a shortlist. A daily record is proof that dedicated, intentional gratitude improves quality of life. Your journal entry may take the following format.

Fig.6.1 Journal sample

A tip to journaling successfully is to focus on pouring your thoughts on paper as opposed to writing "well." Take some time to think about the things to which you are grateful. Be as descriptive as possible.

Schedule a Gratitude Visit

If you have someone to whom you feel you feel grateful, visit them. This exercise will help you purposefully express your gratitude. Let the person know that they are important to you in this journey.

Make a Gratitude Jar

In this exercise, you must place the jar strategically so that you are reminded to be grateful throughout the day, if not twice a day. You may choose to place it beside the bed, or near your toothbrush in the bathroom. You can also choose to decorate the jar with attractive features that remind you to be grateful.

Laugh Out Loud

If you find yourself stressed, or having negative thoughts, burst into laughter for a complete minute. Laughing releases feel-good hormones that relax you. This is an excellent way to distract yourself from sudden unwelcome thoughts and emotions. If you feel happy amid a strife-ridden moment, do not hesitate to indulge in happiness. Celebrate the minor achievements to motivate you toward the bigger goals.

Make a Daily Goal

Decide daily to be grateful for someone or something. If you woke up and went for a twenty-minute run, choose to be thankful for that fete. Being deliberate about gratitude forces us to be more receptive to all the things in life that we, in our ignorance, fail to be thankful for. Writing down your gratitude goals daily, helps you assess your improvement for the week, and perhaps carry forward that emotion for the better part of the coming week.

Find a Gratitude Buddy

Find a companion to help you discuss what you are grateful for daily. It may be a friend, family member, or even a support group. You may open up to one another to fully express thankfulness.

Reduce Your Complaints

It is necessary to give complaints because it is valuable feedback; however, remain mindful of why, and how often you complain. Giving a compliment for every complaint is a brilliant way to keep the scales balanced. Like every other exercise, note down every complaint and compliment you make, and in the evening, assess your day. This exercise will help keep you attuned to your mental health.

Act of Kindness

If you have had someone- besides your friends, and family- who you like, maybe your professor or your doctor, or the local fire department, write them a thank you note expressing their value in the community. These people may not necessarily receive gratitude for their services, and this is your chance to toss them a bone. Writing this thank-you note not only makes the recipient feel good but also remind the sender how incredibly fortunate you are to have them.

Gratitude Prompts

The goal of this exercise is to name three things to which you are grateful. For example; I am grateful for three colors. I am grateful for three textures; I am grateful for three sounds I hear, and so on. You can start, stop, and continue this exercise at any time. Really open up your senses and emotions to get the best out of this test.

Make a Collage

A gratitude collage helps you visualize the things for which you are grateful. Perhaps take pictures of things that you are thankful for, and at the end of the week, take a look at your college paying keen attention to how you feel about it. The more you practice this exercise, the more you will notice the things that you are grateful for.

Extensive research conducted with a group suffering from depression showed that those who practiced gratitude exercises improved faster. Gratitude is said to build emotional resilience. Meditation helps us focus our minds toward the people and things to whom we are truly grateful. Many Buddhist monks start their days and gatherings with a gratitude meditation. These meditation exercises are quick to learn and available online.

It is, however, noteworthy to say that gratitude is not an instant healer. It will not forever vanish your mental anguish and emotional strife. Therefore, do not expect a miracle. These exercises work in reminding us to accept reality and highlight the positive aspects of said reality. Gratitude exercises are a way of expressing positive thoughts towards ourselves and the world around us.

Gratitude can change your personality. Recovering from trauma can be a daunting experience because the mind undergoes reconstruction from the demolition it has continuously endured.

During this reconstruction, you rediscover yourself in a new light. You may no longer go back to your previous life but, instead, reborn into a different one where you are more aware of the many small miracles of life and are grateful for them. You may find yourself to be less materialistic while you had initially been very vain. You might become more spiritual, while initially, the notion of an eternal presence seemed far-fetched.

Daily practice of gratitude exercises helps you keep your vibration high. It is the most obvious yet overlooked technique to get what you want. There is no limit to how grateful you can be in one day. For example, if your goal is to be happy, instead of thinking about how strenuous your life is at the moment, or how depressed you have been lately, focus on being appreciative of the experiences you have had and a daily renewed opportunity at life. Harness the power of gratitude to realize your desires.

Chapter 7: Thriving Mode

Narcissistic abuse is an emotional or psychological abuse directed by a narcissist onto another person. Primarily, it is focused on psychological and emotional abuse, but there are other forms of narcissistic abuse, such as sexual, physical, and financial. What causes this disorder is not known but could be triggered by environmental factors, genetics, and neurobiology.

For one to recover from narcissistic abuse, understanding which form narcissistic abuse exhibit and its effects are critical. Narcissistic abuse comes in the form of obsession with your mistakes, ignoring narcissist's actions, feeling worthless, devaluing your contributions, disconnect from your own needs and wants, idealizing the narcissist, and obsession on making the narcissist happy among many others.

Even once you realize the effects, it's not easy to overcome this situation since most people don't know what to do. But it is important that one gets out to rediscover a sense of self and take control of his/her life. Below is a compilation of ways one can use to overcome the effects of narcissistic abuse and getting their life back:

Set Boundaries

There is a common saying, out of sight, out of mind. When you see someone, who reminds you of something, it will be difficult to move on or disrupt the healing process. Therefore, it's the best way of overcoming narcissistic abuse if you can physically get away. Any memory of the past with the narcissist will trigger the pain and will slow down the recovery process. You may even want to consider blocking them on your phone, email, and any other ways of interactions like social media. Also, do not stalk their profiles.

Let's say it's not possible for you to physically get yourself out of their environment, possibly because of your work or other genuine reasons, there is still a technique you can employ which doesn't involve you not seeing or being close to the narcissist. This technique is called "grey rock." How this works is that while you interact with him/her, you remain mentally and emotionally disengaged, and by doing this, it gives them nothing to feed on. Although you might be hurting inside, do not let it show. Once you are in a place where you are alone, you can do whatever brings you relief. Screams, cry, and cuss comes to my mind, pretty good idea, right?

A different way you can set a boundary is by practicing how to use a word NO. You do want to be agreeing to everything is being said. Other people must notice your stand when it comes to some matters. This will help hugely, not only by making others to give you their respect but also will help you to build true confidence and self-respect. The boundary should function as a cell wall. A cell wall keeps the important nutrients in and excretes the toxic substances out. Be very selective of who you let in.

It should be clear that the bottom line of setting these boundaries is a way of taking care of yourself. Limits make others aware of what to expect from us and definitely what to expect from them on how they treat us. When we communicate our boundaries crystal clear, it's very natural for people to respect them. However, some will do all they can to resist our efforts. They may ignore, blame, and try to manipulate, or even physically hurt us. If this kind of setback occurs you may want to re-evaluate the boundaries which are not being respected and consider other options and take action.

Be Assertive

To overcome the abuse of the narcissist, you may not want to be aggressive or passive. One way to be assertive is by learning to use temporary reactions to handle verbal abuses. For example, "I'll do it my way." Being passive, like ignoring conflict and anger empower the narcissist. Narcissists see this as a weakness and a chance to gain more control and power over you.

A narcissist hardly takes into account any of their evil and illegal actions. They deny the mistake and blame you for it, no remorse whatsoever, and have extreme gratification in causing pain and suffering to others. Their goal is to destroy and cause suffering and pain. The intention is to gain more control over you and continue to increase domination while developing dependency, shame, and doubt in you. When you understand this, it gives you more power to overcome the abuse.

A narcissist is a bully and will make you feel responsible for his behaviors. Do not blame yourself for anything; you have nothing to do with the abuses. Therefore, never feel any guilt because his expectations can never be met no matter how hard you may try. He derives the abuses from his insecurities, and you are only accountable for how you respond. For example, you may not want to respond by trying to rationalize, deny or excuse his abuses. It is a lie to believe that he will improve or stop the behaviors in the future.

All the behaviors of a narcissist call for you to react assertively to put him to his corner. For example, learn more about narcissism and share the information with him. Explain his conduct, reasons, and perhaps the motivations for different behaviors to him. You have to plan well for this on how and when to do this and communicate without being emotional. Another way is facing the abuse with pure confidence because your self-esteem will get destroyed if you allow the abuse. Stand your ground and remain calm as you speak up for yourself as you put on check the emotions.

Know Your Rights

Knowing your rights is very important. When you are aware of your rights, you feel entitled to something and that people must respect it. You command respect from people and let them know that you expect them to treat you in a certain manner. These rights may include: The right to be respected, do not be forced to have sex when you decline, right to privacy, right to opinions, and feelings. When one is exposed to abuse for a long time, his/her self-esteem will slowly diminish, and self-confidence risks being destroyed as well. For an individual who has been in a long-term abuse and has suffered from low self-esteem and low self-confidence, below are ways on how one can re-establish themselves to gain self-confidence:

- Make one list of your strengths and another list of your achievements. You can get your close and supportive friend or caring relative to help you create these two lists. After that, you keep these lists in a safe place where you can read them through every morning as you wake up to a new day.
- Pay close attention to your body hygiene: Take a shower, trim your nails, and shave your hair or brush, and so on.
- Wear smart clothes that make you feel nice about yourself. Ironed outfit, for example, rather than crumpled ones.
- Exercise on a regular basis. Register membership at the gym so you can attend sessions in your spare time or simply go for morning or evening nature walks.
- Make sure you get enough natural sleep. It's best to go to bed early and wake up early in the morning rather than sleep late and wake up late in the morning hours.
- Make your environment conducive. For instance, make you the living space comfortable, clean, and attractive.
- Do things that you love and enjoy doing. You can watch movies, listen to your favorite playlist of music, ride a bike, or swimming. Anything which lifts your spirit and makes you feel good and happy.
- Think positive about yourself. Despite all the challenges and problems you might be going through now, remind yourself that you are special someone and valuable.

- Eat healthy food. Make sure you have a balanced diet in your meals and make the moments special. Switch off the TV, set your table, and enjoy your nice meal.
- Avoid people or places that treat you bad.

Be Strategic

You need to have a strategy on how you are going to come around these abuses. Figure out what you specifically want, your limits, and the power you have in the relationship. You should keep in mind that a narcissist person is highly defensive. There are several strategies you can employ for this purpose. Let's take a look at some of the strategies:

Check for Abuse

Except when the person is emotionally or physically abusive, this should help. If you are being abused, the first thing you should do is explore why it is hard for you to exit the relationship. It doesn't matter the cause, but the reality is the abuser is totally responsible for his/her actions.

Check Your Silence

When our self-esteem has been destroyed, we occasionally resort to being silent during an argument. However, we need to find a voice if things are to get any better. Silence is a way of coping with sadness or anger.

Check Your Anger

Anger is a form of protective measure when faced with an indifferent situation. However, we need to put it on check since they cut us off from information.

Check for Their Willingness to Change

If your partner is ready to work with you, then that is a big plus in an effort to improving the relationship. The easiest way to do this is by seeking help from a therapist.

Be Aware of Manipulation

Narcissists are so manipulative people, and they do whatever it takes to get what they want.

Honesty to Yourself

Probably the only reason you are still holding on is hoping for the change. But there comes a point you need to be honest to yourself and admit you have tried all you can with no avail. So move on already!

Be Educative

The estimated number of individuals with narcissistic disorders, based on research varies widely. Moreover, the insight people have about the narcissistic disorder, and the features of narcissistic differ a lot. You need to be aware that they exist. Hence you have to inform yourself on how to recognize them. It is because of their charming behavior which they use to conceal their narcissistic behaviors, which most people find it hard to see or realize in the beginning. This is because they do not know what to look for, also how these narcissistic behaviors impact negatively on their lives.

There is a lot of good information out there. Therefore, you only have to read as much as possible, to inform yourself about this disorder, and find for yourself which insights connect well with how you are feeling.

There is also research that shows narcissists have got neurological deficits that affect interpersonal reactions. The best way to perhaps help yourself here is to educate the narcissist like a kid. Find a way to explain how their behaviors impact negatively on others. Provide encouragement and incentives for different behavior. You may have to plan how you are going to communicate this without being emotional.

Confront Abuse Effectively

This is a very important step to take. It is one way to salvage your self-esteem and confidence. Allowing abuse to continue for a long time damages your self-esteem. This should not mean you pick a fight or argue with a narcissist. It is a waste of your time and energy to argue over the facts with the abuser. They do not care about the facts but only interested in justifying their actions and being right. Verbal arguments and the exchange of words with anger can easily escalate to fights, which can drain and damage you. This way nothing is gained; you can only end up being hurt and feeling more victimized and hopelessness.

Arguing is as ineffective as making threats or pleading with the abuser to understand you. For example, making threats that you can never implement may lead to retaliation. Do not make a threat you know you cannot enforce. It is more effective and easy to set boundaries which when not respected, lead to direct consequences. Also, with pleading, is a sign of weakness, which abusers despise in themselves and others. This may make them react dismissively in disgust or contempt.

Confronting the abuser, therefore, must be purposeful and should only serve to show your stand. It has to be a way of speaking up for yourself, which calls for you to do it with a clear mind and calmly. You can only manage this by setting boundaries to protect your emotions, mind, and body.

Have Consequences

It is possible that after you set your boundaries, they are ignored. For this reason, it is important to clearly communicate the consequences and invoke them accordingly. However, you also need to set healthy boundaries that are based on mutual respect. It is important to recognize violations as they are, as this will help you to create boundaries where your feelings and needs are respected.

It is also important not to set boundaries that you are unwilling to keep. You can be sure the narcissist will rebel against these boundaries and test how far you can go. You need to make sure that every broken boundary is followed up with the consequence specified. If you fail to do this, you are sending a message that you are not keen on these boundaries, and therefore you will not be taken seriously. It is really up to you to stand tall for this to be successful as the narcissist will make an attempt to manipulate you since he/she is threatened by you trying to take control of your life because he/she is used to being the one in power and calling the shots.

Having consequences is, therefore, without debate very useful and helpful in trying to cope with the abuses of the narcissist as long as you stand firm to the set boundaries and specified consequences. The consequences, for example, may inform you take necessary action such as getting out of the relationship with the narcissist as a result of certainly broken set boundaries. This means it would have eventually helped you to convince yourself that it's the best call to leave for your health and safety.

Get Support and Purpose Elsewhere

Support is necessary if you are to respond effectively to abuse. Without support, it is easy to languish in self-doubt and eventually succumb to narcissist's abusive disinformation. Support is essential as you may get pushback and rebellion when you stand up against the abuses. You will need tools to defend and protect yourself and help lift your self-worth, which will alleviate how you feel whether you choose to stay or leave.

If you decide to stay in a relationship with the narcissist, you need to be honest about yourself, for example, about what you can or can't change or expect. A narcissist is not someone you can be sure things will change, and start caring or values you. Therefore, you will have to look for emotional support elsewhere.

Spend time with individuals who will be honest with you and give you a true reflection of who you really are. This will help you maintain perspective and avoid falling prey into narcissist's manipulations and distortions. In addition, they will help you validate how you feel and your thoughts. Making new friendships will also help. Narcissists will isolate you from other people to better control you and have power over you. In this case, you may want to invest more time in reviving lapsed friendships or creating new relationships.

You can also involve yourself in activities such as volunteering in your neighborhood or at work, which makes use of your abilities and talents, allowing you to make your contributions. This will definitely help you to feel good about yourself instead of looking into someone else to make you feel good.

Trust Your Intuition

This is a point where we do a reasonable post-mortem analysis, and we start to take responsibility that part of you knew what will happen but disregarded it. Maybe at some early point in the relationship, you had a certain feeling in your stomach. Perhaps the things they said or the way they acted did not add up. Ask yourself what reason you had that time to ignore your intuitive hint. It could be because you really wanted the relationship to work, or maybe their acts of "love" filled that space inside your soul, avoid possibly left behind from childhood experiences.

If you never experienced true love as a child, specifically from your parents or guardians, it is normal to seek fulfillment of love now as a grown-up. However, it is a vulnerability which a narcissist may notice and uses it to gain control over your life. Treat your intuition as a friend, and the more you trust and listen to it, the stronger you become and realize your self-worth.

Narcissisms are not only experienced in our love relationships, we also find them at home, places of work, our schools, and in our friendships. Therefore, we interact with these situations more often than you may think, only that maybe we don't notice them. It is for this reason that we learn features of narcissisms to recognize when we stumble upon them and equip ourselves with tools to overcome their abuses, such as the ones highlighted above. Remember the person with conscientiousness and sensitivity is the healthy one in the relationship, while the one with a feeling of entitlement and treat another person with disrespect, is normally emotionally unhealthy.

Narcissists' central play is to destroy your confidence and self-esteem. They do this by revoking our emotions, which exposes our vulnerability. It is, therefore, helpful not to show our emotions when interacting with them as they use opportunities like this to get into us and manipulate. Building your self-confidence will help shield you from these abuses. Refer to the ways above on how to build or re-establish your self-confidence.

Chapter 8 - Getting into a New Relationship

You might be well equipped mentally and emotionally to recognize the apparent warnings that you are starting a toxic relationship with a narcissist. But unfortunately, so many people are unaware of these red flags and will find themselves easily attracted to these toxic people.

The good news is that a narcissist relationship will eventually end. Narcissists tend to tire off their victims once they are through exploiting them of their support and resources, such as money or care. They will then leave your life without as much warning, just like the way they entered.

The break up will leave you devastated, but with the time, you will appreciate their absence in your life. Once you heal from the breakup, you need to focus on moving on with your life. Here are some of the signs that will help you to know that you are finally over a narcissist relationship, and you are ready to date again.

Signs You Are Ready for a New Relationship

You Don't Think About Them Anymore

Once you stop thinking and caring about your last love, then it is an excellent sign that finally, you are over them. At the initial stages of your break up, you will be preoccupied with them, and as such, you might even be tempted to reach out for a reunion. However, with time, you gain a new perspective, and you will find no reason to pay any attention to them.

Besides, once you get them out of your mind, it could mean you can comfortably meet them or hear about them through your mutual friends without having those past feelings rushing back. You find yourself not caring about them anymore.

You Have No Hatred for Them

Any relationship break up usually comes with a lot of conflicting emotions, more so if you break up with a narcissist. You may have intense hatred towards them, especially whenever you remember all the wrong things they did to hurt you. At times, however, you find yourself yearning to let them back into your life. All these conflicting feelings can be confusing, and you might be left in a dilemma of whether to move on or go back to them. Relationship experts advise you take some time off any relationship until you have dealt conclusively with these conflicting emotions. The day you realize you don't hate your former partner anymore is the day you are entirely free. You can then move on with your life.

When You Can Open up Freely

In most cases, you may find it challenging to open up about your abusive past relationships. It could be because you are afraid of the shame and stigma that can come from such revelations. However, it is a good idea to open up to someone you trust about your past. This is an essential step in the healing process. It is still advice able to let go of your abuser and move on, never looking back. When you find yourself ready to open up about your past abusive relationship, then it could be a great sign that you are finally ready to move on.

Besides, opening up could mean more than just telling a close friend. Where stalking or domestic abuse is involved, it is safe for you to engage the authorities. Although you may feel you are betraying your ex, it is good to submit a police report for your safety. When you realize speaking up about your abuse is the right thing to do and you no longer feel bad or guilty about it, then you know you are finally free. If you can successfully do this, then it means you are entirely free from your past relationship, and you are now ready to date again.

You Don't Stalk Them Anymore

After any break up you may be tempted to stalk your ex, primarily through social media. The temptation to find out what they are up to can be particularly overwhelming. Curiosity can never harm you, but if you find yourself curious about your narcissist ex's daily activities, then there is a cause to worry.

A narcissist can take advantage of your curious nature to pretend to be sad or anxious and suffering knowing too well that you are monitoring their lives. This is how they will hook you and make you feel responsible for their emotions.

But if you no longer worry about what they are up to or who they hang out with, then it is a good sign that finally, you are over them, and you are now ready to move on with your life.

You Don't Feel Wrong About Your past Experiences

You may always be tempted to judge yourself harshly for failing to see through the lies of your narcissistic ex. You may have regrets of ignoring the apparent warnings that could have quickly helped you to know you were in an abusive relationship. Still, you may be bitter at yourself for being so dumb and not running away from your abuser. All these blames are a sign that you are not entirely healed, and you may not be ready for a new relationship.

Narcissists are skillful at manipulating others, and they mainly target successful and confident people to boost their image. It is no use blaming yourself for their actions.

Once you no longer feel dumb and doubtful about your critical thinking skills, then it is high time you go out on a date with someone else.

You Have No Fear of Falling for a Similar Person Again

The first initial days after your break up may make you so fearful of meeting new people. You may end up being too vigilant and always looking out lest you meet another person who will treat you as bad as your ex.

Once you stop the unnecessary caution of looking out for a narcissist in every other person you meet, then it could be a great sign that you are now ready to move on with your life. This means you can freely interact with other people without having that nagging thought that they may possess the same qualities as those of your ex.

When you go for dates with a new guy, and you realize that your mind is free from any negative emotions associated with your narcissist ex, it is a good sign that you are finally over him and can now settle with someone else.

You Take Care of Yourself

Narcissist abuse can wreak havoc on you, both physically and emotionally. Going through such an experience could mean you were so stressed up that you failed to take good care of yourself. As a result, you might have needed up losing or putting on too much weight. You may also have ignored the good beneficial routines that could keep you fit and healthy such as regular workouts and eating healthy food. This will result in your body responding to the negative changes, and you may have a break out of acne or even complicated diseases such as heart attacks and diabetes. As a result of stress, you may end up looking so old, sad, and haggard or so thin or fat.

However, once you are out of the toxic environment, you will find yourself taking good care of your body again. You may start going to the gym again. You are also more aware of the kind of food you consume, and you make a conscious effort to choose healthy food over the unhealthy ones. Your body gets more robust, and your physical appearance is much improved. This could be a great sign that you are over your abusive relationship, and you are ready to start all over again.

You Are Ready to Take the Risk Again

It is often said that great love and great achievements involve some significant risks. You may experience some nervousness at the thought of dating back, especially after a break up from an abusive relationship. This, however, is a normal feeling. But if you are still convinced that your next relationship might not work out or may end up becoming an exact copy of the last one, then you probably need more time for yourself to heal fully.

The truth is all relationships carry with them some element of risk. The day you find inner strength and have come up with a solid foundation of independence, then it is an excellent sign that you are ready to move on.

But if you are not sure whether to on or not, then wait for a while before you make that move. Whenever you are in doubt, it is advisable to talk to someone you trust. This could be your closest friend or your counselor. But once you have cleared all your fears and doubts, then it is a great moment for you to meet new people.

You Genuinely Want to Start a New Relationship

An additional sign that you are ready for a new relationship after a narcissist relationship is that you know within yourself that you genuinely want to start one. However, if you only desire to start a new relationship because you are under a lot of pressure or you feel inadequate and lonely, then it is advisable not to start one at this point. The relationship may end up being so unfulfilling and empty.

If you want to avoid further hurts, then choose to wait for that special someone who truly complements you and makes you feel happy and complete once again.

However, finding this ideal person may require a lot of time and patience on your part. Once you truly feel you want to start a new relationship for the right reasons, then it is time you find that unique person whom you truly connect with and wan as a partner.

Redefining Sexy After a Narcissistic Relationship

You may have encountered several pictures of what society perceives to be attractive people in magazines or TV commercials. But have you ever paused to consider the meaning of being sexy? Could it be that someone somewhere is setting specific standards to the rest of us on what sexiness and attractiveness entails?

After coming through an abusive relationship, it is normal for you to be obsessed with being sexy and attractive once again. However, you should be more careful about how you go about this. This is because sexy doesn't always mean safe. Some men may take advantage of your vulnerability and low self-esteem under the wrong assumption that you will feel grateful that any man would be attracted to you.

Besides, you should know that being sexy and attractive goes beyond the looks and all that makes up the "aura." There is an incredibly sexy and attractive person inside you who is screaming to be let out. Here is how you can redefine sexiness in your unique world and make the whole world have more than a precursory glance at you.

Don't Think You Are Unattractive; Make Yourself Attractive Instead

Learn to develop the right attitude about your attractiveness. This is an essential step in redefining your sexiness once again. If you think of yourself as attractive, then others will follow suit and find you attractive also. The change will happen at that moment; you make a conscious decision of thinking and making yourself beautiful.

Don't Let Your past Relationship Affect Your Current Life

You kill your sexiness with fear if you carry the baggage of your past failed relationship into your present life. The pain and heartbreak you suffered in the past belong to the past. You need to deal with them conclusively for you to move into a new life of happiness. You need to learn from where you have been and be determined to make your current life better emotionally. Dealing with your past decisively builds up your confidence level and makes you charming both to yourself and your friends

Find Your Confidence

No one is as attractive and sexy as an overly confident person. You need to believe in yourself, get to know who you are. Once you master this, you will go about your daily business, exuding some attractiveness to those around you. You possess an aura of mystery and send the message that you are an exciting person. If you successfully manage to build your confidence level, then most people will find you very attractive and would want to be associated with you. This is one great way of making friends.

Dress Well and Give Yourself a Treat

Your choice of clothing can significantly enhance your physical features. You have to find out what clothes and colors fit you the best. Determine which clothes make you look great and attractive.

When you dress sharply, you tend to be more confident and attractive. Once you have dressed up, take yourself out for a date, preferably to an expensive restaurant that fits your class and status. Be comfortable with dining alone, and this will send attractive vibes to anyone watching you.

Maintain the Right Posture

One of the s most attractive thing in a man is his posture. Your posture and the way you generally present yourself sends a subtle message to the whole world on who you indeed are. Make intentional eye contact with people around you. Give out random smiles and stand tall, shoulders relaxed.

Learn to practice standing tall to communicate confidence in your brain, which will trigger off your feelings to feel the same.

Learn the Skills of a Good Romance

Romance is not as complicated as many people think. It could be as simple as looking at your partner's eyes to find out what is going on inside them. Romance can also be the choice of the words you use when communicating with your partner during the day or at night, either through word of mouth or texts and calls. When you take your time to go into the depths of your heart and select the right words to say to your lover, it can create a natural feeling of romance. Once you master the art of romance, you end up being the most romantic man or woman around, and many find passionate people to be lovely.

Love Yourself and Your Life

You need to find what goes on inside you and your heart. You are a precious person who has so much to offer to oneself and the rest of the world. Create a great interest in your life, which motivates you to keep waking up every morning. Develop a sense of purpose that prompts you to find out why you exist and how you can bring a difference to your world.

Learn to take full control of your life to spend your time doing the things that make you happy and which can have a positive impact on the lives of others. Learn to listen to your inner feelings and strive to satisfy your desires and drives. Once you learn to t love yourself and your life, you succeed in making yourself an incredibly attractive and sexy person.

How to Become Your Own Source of Happiness?

They say you are responsible for your satisfaction. And the truth of this statement cannot be gainsaid. Your satisfaction is actually within your control. You should avoid letting your happiness be control by external forces. Instead, use the following tips to create your happiness:

Make Yourself a Priority

You should show yourself some real love by prioritizing on what makes you happy. This shouldn't be random but should be a routine practice that you do regularly each day. Get out and give yourself a treat for no reason once in a while. Put on your favorite music and dance to it. Go for pedicure and manicure. You should also go for shopping and get yourself that fancy expensive dress you dream of. Engage in activities that make you fulfilled and refreshes and recharges your battery to make you happy.

Do the Little Things You Love More Often

You don't have to do fancy stuff for you to be happy. Sometimes you find happiness in the small things you do. It could be a sip from your favorite coffee brand or that delicious meal, which puts a cheer on your face. It could be watching your favorite program or movie. Or it could be that yoga exercises which you find so relaxing and therapeutic. Find those little things that make you happy and do them more.

Challenge Yourself by Doing Something New

You need to break your monotonous, boring routines and once in a while do something new. This will not only give you happiness but will also renew your energy. Try something new which you have never tried before. It could be that hike across the hill or sky diving. Go for activities that set off your adrenaline.

Get Enough Sleep

Sleep is vital in improving your mood, happiness, and self-control. Sleep enables your brain to recharge and get rid of toxic by-products of the healthy brain neural function. Getting enough sleep ensures you wake up feeling energized, focused, and stress-free.

Do the Workouts

Exercises improve your mood and contribute immensely to your happiness. Studies show that peoples who engage in regular workouts are far happier, productive, and successful in achieving their life goals. Exercise also helps to limit impulsivity.

How to Stay Single and Blessed

You may be struggling to remain comfortable after a breakup. However, happiness is not necessarily tied to your soulmate. It is actually possible to be single and happy. You need to learn how to be happy without depending on the status of your relationship. The following tips will help you to be alone and happy.

Learn to Do Things on Your Own

Most people are afraid of carrying out their normal activities on their own. You need to learn to go shopping by yourself. Go out for movies or dinner alone. Learn to enjoy your life by yourself. Your happiness is your personal choice, and it is not tied to someone else.

Develop Other Relationships

You need to foster other meaningful relationships with family or friends. It is not a condition for you to be romantically involved in order to be happy. Family and friends can be a great source of support and happiness. Create more time for them because they offer the most exceptional support whenever you face life's challenges.

Meet New People

You need to cultivate the necessary skills that enable you to meet up with new people without necessarily having a romantic date. Talk to other people but, more importantly, listen to what they have to say on a wide range of issues. You need to step out of your comfort zone and intentionally set up meetings with new people.

Treat Yourself

While you are single, you should maintain a positive self-image. Go out shopping and get yourself new outfits. Get a fresh pedicure or a manicure, spend time in a spa, or get yourself that excellent massage. Ensure you do beautiful things to yourself more frequently. You are a wonderful individual who deserves the best

Maintain a Supportive, Positive Company

Don't spend too much time alone. Spend more time with people who make you happy. Join a club if necessary. Moreover, ensure you are in the right company of people who resonates with some positive energy. Get support from people you can trust and who are not judgmental about your single status.

Conclusion

Thank you for making it through to the end *Narcissistic Abuse Healing Guide: Follow the Ultimate Narcissists Recovery Guide, Heal and Move on From an Emotional Abusive Relationship! Recover From Narcissism or Narcissist Personality Disorder!* Let us hope that it was information and able to provide you and your loves ones with all the tools you need to overcome any instances of narcissistic abuse. By finishing this book, you will be able to possess the mastery that you seek in dealing with any narcissists around you, and how to feel better even after suffering as a narcissistic victim.

We have gone through the success stories of narcissistic abuse and the understanding of narcissistic personality disorder. This book has offered easy-to-use but very powerful and effective techniques for tackling any signs of narcissistic abuse. You are now familiar with the concept of pseudo personality. You have further learnt about the strategies necessary for dealing with pseudo personality, including how you can acknowledge that you have a pseudo personality.

For this book to work for you, it is vital that you encompass all the advice and techniques you have read herein. It may not be in the order that I listed them in this book, but you must use all of them for maximum benefits. You are now aware that you must know and decide to overcome any memory challenges, regardless of the cause. The next thing you would want to do is put in a request for what you want. By purchasing this book, you will get the opportunity to start over a life that is full of activeness, awareness, and memorization of important experiences in life.

Finally, if you found this book useful in any way, an honest review is always appreciated!

www.ingramcontent.com/pod-product-compliance
Lightning Source LLC
Chambersburg PA
CBHW072001070526
44583CB00015B/1286